Navigating Teacher Licensure Exams

Navigating Teacher Licensure Exams offers practical, empirically sourced insights into the high-stakes licensure exams required in most states for teacher certification. This unique resource foregrounds the experiences of diverse preservice teachers, including teachers of color, to understand how they organize their preparation efforts, overcome self-doubt and anxiety, and navigate the high-pressure space of this important testing event. By situating these exams within their social and psychological contexts, presenting real-life cases of success and failure, and confronting innate perceptions of standardized tests, this book provides essential and highly practical support for preservice teachers, teacher educators, and departmental resource libraries.

Emery Petchauer is Associate Professor in the Departments of English and Teacher Education and Coordinator of the English Education Program at Michigan State University, USA.

Navigating Teacher Licensure Exams

Success and Self-Discovery on the High-Stakes Path to the Classroom

EMERY PETCHAUER

Routledge
Taylor & Francis Group

NEW YORK AND LONDON

First published 2019
by Routledge
52 Vanderbilt Avenue, New York, NY 10017

and by Routledge
2 Park Square, Milton Park, Abingdon, Oxon, OX14 4RN

Routledge is an imprint of the Taylor & Francis Group, an informa business

Contents from the following articles have been reprinted, with permission, in
this book:

Baker-Doyle, Kira J. and Emery Petchauer. "Rumor Has It: Investigating Teacher
Licensure Exam Networks." *Teacher Education Quarterly 42*, no. 3 (2015): 3–32.

Petchauer, Emery. "I Will Not Fail: How African American Preservice Teachers
Succeed on Licensure Exams After Initially Failing." *The Educational Forum 82*,
no. 4 (2018): 443–460.

Petchauer, Emery. "Teacher Licensure Exams and Black Teacher Candidates:
Toward New Theory and Promising Practice." *Journal of Negro Education 81*,
no. 3 (2012): 252–67.

Petchauer, Emery. "'Slaying Ghosts in the Room': Identity contingencies, teacher
licensure testing events, and African American preservice teachers." *Teachers
College Record 116*, no. 7 (2014): 1–40.

Petchauer, Emery. "Passing as White: Race, Shame, and Success in Teacher
Licensure Testing Events for Black Preservice Teacher." *Race, Ethnicity, and
Education 18*, no. 6 (2015): 834–57.

Library of Congress Cataloging-in-Publication Data
A catalog record for this title has been requested

ISBN: 978-0-8153-4806-1 (hbk)
ISBN: 978-0-8153-4807-8 (pbk)
ISBN: 978-1-351-16816-8 (ebk)

Typeset in Avenir and Dante
by Swales & Willis Ltd

Contents

Figures and Tables

Figures

Tables

Preface

There are some topics we choose to study. Others choose us.

I took my own licensure exams going through a teacher education program in Illinois. I then took another set of them when I applied for a license in California. I remember coming home from student teaching when the envelope with my English content score arrived in the mail. I was on the cusp of so much: finishing my capstone teaching internship, graduating, and starting a career. I applied nationally for jobs and already had interviews lined up. Standing in front of the table where my roommates and I piled our mail, I knew the contents of this sealed envelope could stop it all. My mind circled around these possibilities as my fingers tore open the envelope and unfolded the creased paper. I skipped all the text and even the numbers. I scanned for the only word that mattered: PASS.

Relief.

Years later, after teaching high school and finishing graduate school, I started my career as a scholar and teacher educator. I saw teacher candidates tear open their own envelopes (or open emails) and scan for that same word. Some found it. Others didn't. Some who failed the exam were committed and capable emerging educators who performed well in my classes. These weren't the teacher candidates who the exams were supposed to screen out, were they? This puzzled me. What was going on? Why did the results on the licensure exam report differ so much from what was happening in class? What was happening behind those testing walls when the door shut? What went on in students' minds and hearts after exam proctors told them, "you can open your test booklet now"? I had navigated similar exams, but my experiences mapped out only partially onto my students' experiences. As a faculty member in a small teacher education program, I was not in a position to ignore this question, pursue it only in the abstract, or overlook the pressing implications it had on the lives of young adults I cared deeply about.

The strongest lesson I learned from my graduate school professor Michael K. Ponton is that a scholar should be able to ask a question and find suitable answers to it. This process doesn't have to be an individual and isolated one, but a person who holds the highest degree awarded by a system of education should have developed the desire, initiative, resourcefulness, and persistence to ask the question and see the answer through. From this stance, a doctoral degree isn't about a certain level of smarts; it's about developing certain qualities and traits to adequately see the answers through – and, to a lesser extent, some smarts to go along with them.

This book is the product of roughly ten years of trying to see the answer through with teacher licensure exams. Within this decade is a six-year window of time working consistently with preservice teachers to pass their exams – the students who often didn't find the word PASS on their exam reports. These efforts entailed organizing and facilitating workshops, working one-on-one with some students, debriefing and discussing their experiences after taking the exam, celebrating victories, and trying to regroup after failures.

Within this six-year window is smaller sequence of four years during which I conducted a research study alongside these efforts, exploring students' experiences with the exam. This study and my thinking about the topic evolved in a few ways over time. Early on, I was thinking mostly about licensure exams as an individual process and what students believed about their own capabilities. The interviews I conducted with students reflected this focus. As the study progressed, I started considering how ideas and experiences from social psychology – like stereotype threats and identity contingencies – played into licensure exam experiences and outcomes. These frameworks pushed me to start considering the exam as a collective experience that could implicate group identities rather than an individual experience. I also started thinking of the exam as a "test event" – like a big, high-pressure game people put on the calendar and train for. This new thinking influenced my data collection techniques, leading me to conduct focus group interviews rather than individual ones and apply different interpretive lenses. In the last stages of this study, I started asking questions about students' affective/emotional experiences with the exam, the "space" of testing, and the advice networks through which they developed important ideas about themselves and their licensure exam.

Though still interviewing students in groups, these new priorities further shifted the questions I asked, led me to administer a survey, and pushed me into different ways of interpreting responses. In this final stage of the study, I also moved beyond students in my own teacher education program and partnered with a colleague at a different institution to explore these questions in a different context and among her students. (Of course, specific colleagues and research partners helped initiate these shifts too, and I name them specifically in the Acknowledgements section of this book.) In total, 64 students participated in this academic study, most of whom were African American. Though not a glutton for punishment, I also went to take the state-required professional readiness licensure exam in Pennsylvania and Michigan a number of times during this period, separately, on my own. I passed each time, except for once.

Consistent across the evolving stages of the study were interviews with students at different stages of their preparation – especially after taking the exam. In some years, I also went to the exam with students on early Saturday mornings as they traveled together in a group to take the exam. I wanted to understand how they felt at the exam sites and what was happening around them at the exam sites. What were the site administrators and proctors saying? Who else was at the exam site? How did students make sense of these other people? And so on. Most of all, since I had worked with many of these students preparing for the exam, I went as a show of support. On site, I wasn't permitted to enter the actual test room with students, but I interacted with them in the commons areas of these sites and learned a great deal.

Since this was not an abstract topic, thinking about the practical implications of what I was learning – how it could help the people in front of me – was, and remains, on my mind. I was never concerned that helping a preservice teacher to pass their licensure exam (even if they failed it multiple times) might compromise the quality of the teaching profession, a concern occasionally raised by test developers, policy-makers, and journalists. This logic does not hold up to research findings (see Chapter 6).

The final years of the decade that spanned this project have entailed making sense and bringing it to a meaningful end (if there ever is such a thing with a project we invest so much in). In thinking through the "final" rendering, this book changed a great deal. At first, it was shaping up to be devastating critique of teacher licensure exams, especially how they sustain the prevailing whiteness of the teaching profession. Like many people who work in education fields, I am critical of high-stakes standardized exams.

They are overused in schools, put a stranglehold on curricula, and place unnecessary stress on students and teachers, among other things. The exams also have a complicated entanglement to racism and other systems of violence, like the eugenics movement. Education systems would be better off with fewer high-stakes and standardized exams.

But over time while completing this book, I gradually came to accept something I sensed all along but could no longer ignore: a book driven solely by these critiques, while perhaps garnering critical props, would do little to directly support the kinds of preservice teachers that made me start asking questions in the first place. The largely practical, applied stance of this book is a product of this acceptance. This move has pushed me into an uncomfortable space, somewhere between three groups that seldom interact with one another and that take-up rather established positions: education scholars critical of standardized exams, psychometricians who make tests, and the test preparation industry.

The first group critiques high-stakes standardized exams for many reasons: their cultural and racial bias, their roots in the eugenics movement and racist science, their role in limiting opportunities for low-income and students of color, and more. From this stance, licensure exams are tools of oppression that uphold existing inequalities. These scholars are right about many of these points. But the most powerful critique of standardized tests won't do anything to help the teacher on the bubble of a passing score to get over and into the classroom.

The second group exists behind the curtain of test development companies and copyright laws, occasionally responding to critiques but mostly allowing them to exist in a scholarly echo chamber. For this group, standardized tests are rather straightforward technical endeavors, not political battlegrounds for educational justice. If anything, teacher licensure exams weed out underqualified preservice teachers that education programs cannot or will not on their own.

And the third group, the substantial test preparation industry, sidesteps the political and technical dimensions altogether. Freelance tutors, online platforms, and study books full of sample problems respond to the demands this system has put upon preservice teachers, especially those who are unsupported by their education programs. For some preservice teachers, these products and services seem like the only practical way forward, and they make all the difference in success. In other instances, these products are lucrative snake oil made from outdated test questions, tricks, flashy digital platforms, and false guarantees about "cracking the code" of the exam.

Somewhere between these three positions, this space has pushed me to think more deeply about assuming a particular kind of disposition. In *Critical Dispositions: Evidence and Expertise in Education*, Greg Dimitriadis (drawing upon Pierre Bourdieu) treats dispositions as the subjective ways we take-up, work through, and move across the available and oftentimes predictable positions in given fields. The concept of disposition in this context implies flexibility and movement – not the creation of new fields of study or doubling-down as a response to resource scarcity and political polarization. Between the three positions referenced above, I've been pushed to develop a kind of critical-pragmatic disposition in this book: one that holds onto principled critiques, but also knows when to hold them back to make room for pragmatic, urgent solutions for and with the folks who need them – *right now*.

Acknowledgments

At the center of this book are students who shared their experiences with me. This tends to come easy when those experiences are positive – and not so much when they are negative. I extend graduate to each of them, remain inspired by their courage and resolve, and have taken many lessons from them into my own life.

My earliest collaborator in this work was Lynnette Mawhinney, who helped me make small adjustments early on that would make big differences in the end. I am deeply thankful for her friendship, wisdom, and spirit for over a decade now. Decoteau Irby nudged me over and over to think about who this work was for and, specifically, that it should be for preservice teachers and not for scholars like us. He was right, and I'm all the richer from this insight, as well as our friendship that started all the way back in Philly. Whether summarizing decades of social capital research for me in a single text message or nodding along as I tried to make sense of spatial theories, Kira Baker-Doyle helped me turn new theoretical corners in this work. I found much more than a researcher collaborator when I asked her to partner with me a few years into this work. I found a dear friend.

This project has spanned my positions as a faculty member at Lincoln University, Oakland University, and Michigan State University. I've benefited from sharp and generous colleagues at each of these places who keep me moving intellectually. A number of people at these institutions and others have given me direct feedback on this work or been in conversation with me about the politics and practices around licensure exams. I'm grateful to Rene Antron-Gonzalez, Jason Esters, Marybeth Gasman, Alice Ginsberg, Nicholas Hartlep, Rich Milner, Ken Parker, Zizwe Poe, F. Carl

Walton, and York Williams in this regard. In this current season, I appreciate the support of my MSU colleagues in the Department of English and the Department of Teacher Education, especially my English Education colleagues with whom I work most directly and from whom I gain much inspiration: April Baker-Bell, Tamara Butler, Lamar Johnson, Mary Juzwik, Jen VanDerHeide, and Vaughn W. M. Watson. Outside of MSU, I know I can count on Adam Banks, Ed Brockenbrough, Ruth Nicole Brown, Todd Craig, Mike Dando, Tabitha Dell'Angelo, Chris Emdin, Sarah Hobson, Stevie Johnson, Jung Kim, David Kirkland, Ian Levy, Treva Lindsey, Bettina Love, Brian Lozenski, Gholdy Muhammad, Django Paris, Jason Rawls, Yolanda Sealey-Ruiz, Sonia Rosen, and Vajra Watson to keep me inspired, have my back if I need it, or come up with outlandish book titles on out-of-control email threads. A big shout out goes to my fellow Deruters for showing that there is another way: Elizabeth Drame, Dominique Duval-Diop, Decoteau Irby, Laura Porter-field, Jacqueline Robinson-Hunsicker, and Jeff Roman. Since the fall of 1996, Louis Gallien has been and continues to be the mentor I need.

The last leg of this project took place mostly while sitting next to my spouse and partner, Anica Bowe – me typing away at my laptop, she doing the same at hers – and the both of us trading laughter and stealing glances in between, which, in the end, are all more dear to me than anything written in these pages. I'm grateful for her bulletproof joy, enduring faith in me and other people, and most of all that she took a chance and said yes to reggae night.

Part 1

Thinking Differently About Struggle and Support

Introduction

1

What We Need More Than Test Prep

In one of my favorite scenes from the *Lord of the Rings* film, Gandalf, Frodo, and the rest of the Fellowship of the Ring find themselves surrounded by goblins deep in the mines of Moria. As the pack of goblins approaches, a deep rumbling through the mines catches the ugly creatures' attention and sends them scurrying away. Then, it's only silence, as The Fellowship strains to decipher this dark, fading echo through the mines.

"What is this new devilry?" whispers Boromir into the empty stillness.

Gandalf, the old wizard who has been guiding them on the journey, responds in a stern and pensive tone: "A Balrog! A demon of the ancient world. This foe is beyond any of you. Run!"

Dashing from this demon, The Fellowship makes it to the Bridge of Khazad Dum that extends over a deep, dark abyss. So narrow is the 50-foot bridge that the group can only pass in a single line, one at a time. Each of them races over the bridge, except for Gandalf who has let them all pass before him. The wizard stops halfway across the bridge, planting himself between the approaching Balrog and The Fellowship that carries what has caused all this trouble in the first place: the Ring. The *precious* Ring.

A mammoth of fire, shadow, and darkness soon appears before Gandalf at the foot of the bridge. With crimson flying off its shoulders and penetrating through its eyes, the Balrog towers over Gandalf. It wields a flaming sword and a glowing whip of thongs. This won't end well.

The two clash swords, and Gandalf shatters the Barlog's into pieces. "Go back to the shadows!" the old wizard commands from deep in his belly.

Defiant, the ancient demon draws its glowing whip and stomps out onto the thin stone bridge. With Frodo, Aragorn and the others looking over this last stand, Gandalf summons all his strength, thrusts his staff high above his head, and drives it with both hands down into the bridge, belting out one of the most memorable lines from *Lord of the Rings*:

"YOU SHALL NOT PASS!!!"

The stone bridge breaks in half under Gandalf's blow and the Balrog tumbles into the abyss. Its roar fades as the darkness below engulfs its glowing frame. But! The tail of its long whip lashes up, wrapping around Gandalf's ankle and pulling him off the jagged edge of the broken bridge. With The Fellowship watching in horror, their old guide falls into the darkness below.

Unlike in *Lord of the Rings*, there are no wizards, Balrogs, or precious rings on the journey to becoming a teacher. But there are narrow bridges that you must travel and cross over. One of these bridges is the professional licensure exam. Some students sit for these exams and pass without much trouble. Others go through serious preparation and pass with possibly a few bumps along the way. And yet others experience something different altogether. The exam is like the sound of the Balrog was to Boromir: "a new devilry" invented by test companies for the sole purpose of dashing dreams into pieces so they'll fall into the abyss below. For these prospective teachers who might struggle, Gandalf's final command rings true when they think about taking on the exam one more time: *YOU SHALL NOT PASS!*

This book is not a test prep manual. Its chapters do not contain lists of exam questions for drill-and-kill practice with an answer key in the back. Some people find resources such as this useful, but this book is a different kind of tool. You will also not find in these chapters any talk about "cracking the code" of your teacher licensure exam and fool proof strategies guaranteed to make you pass. It's important to know how exams work and be prepared with a set of strategies when you take them, but certification exams are not ancient ciphers with a code to crack. Plus, all people are not the same. Some strategies and approaches that work for the next person might not work for you.

So if this book isn't a test prep manual, what is it? And how can it be of use to you? I can answer these questions by sharing a true story about two students, Shonda and Tammy.

Shonda took the professional readiness (or "basic skills") exam to be admitted into her teacher education program during her sophomore year. In her state, she had to pass a reading, writing, and mathematics exam to be admitted. Shonda didn't study much for these exams but fortunately passed the reading and writing on her first try. The math was another story. Not only did she fail, out of forty questions, she needed to get eleven more right to pass. Yikes. Two months later, she took the math test again. The only difference this time was that she took the computerized version of the exam rather than the paper-based one she had before. Guess what happened? She failed again with the exact same score. The next semester – now into her junior year and the pressure starting to build – she took the math exam yet again. This time, between her second and third sitting for the exam, she did some things differently. First, she got a math education major to meet with her twice a week and help prepare. What they did *not* do is run through pages and pages of math problems in attempt to cover as much ground as possible. They diagnosed a small set of skills on the math exam that Shonda had not mastered, and they focused primarily on those skills. Looking at the overview of the test provided by the test company, they made sure that there was a decent number of these kinds of questions on the exam. Their preparation was an inch wide and a mile deep. Second, they focused not only on mastering those skills but on identifying those exact question types. (Remember, on a math exam, a particular skill can be tested through a variety of question types.) When Shonda went to take the exam for the third time, she first went through the exam and identified each of the question types she had worked on. In other words, instead of avoiding what might have been her weak area, she went directly toward it. This way her new score was sure to reflect the new knowledge that she did not have the previous times she took the exam.

This order of proceeding through the exam wasn't a trick. It was a specific tactic based upon Shonda's individual need and preparation for the exam. When Shonda finished the exam, she didn't have a strong sense that she passed. In fact, taking the exam this time around felt quite similar to the other two times she took it and did not pass. When her score arrived in the mail a few weeks later, she nervously opened the envelope to see if she had gained the eleven points she needed to pass the exam. Reading the score, she saw that she hadn't gained the eleven points. Instead, she had gained thirteen. She not only passed the exam, she exceeded the required score by two points.

There is more to Shonda's story that I'll share in the next chapter. But for the time being, we can see that Shonda passed not from immersing herself in a sea of practice problems, finding the right trick, or through luck. She passed through smart, focused preparation based upon an understanding of her individual needs and through leveraging the resources around her. Resources from this perspective weren't just objects. Resources were also key people and the expertise they held. Also, notice that the time Shonda finally passed the math exam, the experience felt about the same as it did the two times she failed the exam. She was nervous each time, and perhaps a bit more nervous the time she finally passed because the pressure had been mounting. She was in tune with the affective or "feeling dimension" of the experience, but she did not trust that dimension as the only information source to tell her how she would perform. We have much to learn from students like Shonda.

We also have a great deal to learn from people like Tammy. Like Shonda, Tammy had to pass a professional readiness exam in reading, writing, and math to be admitted into her teacher education program. Tammy took all three portions of the exam together the first time. She passed the writing exam by obtaining the passing score right on the mark, and she exceeded the cut-off score for reading by eight points. Again, the math was another story; she was ten points short of passing. She wasted no time and made an appointment at a computerized test center to retake the exam the following month. Instead of sitting back and hoping she would pass on her second attempt, she got busy – very busy, in fact. She made a detailed study plan for herself and found a math professor at her university who would tutor her twice a week. By her own account, Tammy used "every test book in the library" and they covered "every one of the questions" that would be on the exam. Tammy was also concerned with who else in her program was passing and not passing the exam, and if there were key differences within this group. This concern led her to create a survey about the exam that she distributed to other students in her program to see who struggled with the exam more: men or women. Somewhat stereotypically, she concluded that women struggled more with the exam. From this conclusion she reached out to a few other women in her program that were in a similar situation so they could study together.

Tammy was also convinced that there were specific methods necessary for passing the teacher licensure exam and other standardized tests like it. She called these "tricks" and often admitted, "I don't know the trick. And I never did." Tammy also spent a lot of time thinking about herself and all of the pressure she felt she was under to pass the exam: pressure from her family, husband, and due to her stage in life. Some of these pressures related to Tammy's age. She was entering teaching as a second career and was in her 40s, much older than the other students in her program.

Having "learned math about twenty years ago" (as she would say) weighed heavily upon her preparation efforts. Tammy seemed not only concerned with the exam but at times consumed by it.

As you might guess, Tammy did not pass the math exam the second time she took it. In fact, she received the same score she did the first time she took it despite all of her effort. She took it a third time as well and also failed. Her struggles to pass were not due to lack of effort, commitment, or persistence. In fact, Tammy demonstrated great persistence while preparing for the exam, as illustrated by some of the details I've shared above. There were more layers to her situation, however, than just study and persistence: layers relating to how she perceived and made sense of herself and her situation as a middle-aged person and as a woman. Although there is more to Tammy's story that I will cover later in this book, you can see from what I've shared here that preparing to retake the exam was as much about the exam as it was about *her*.

These brief snapshots of Shonda and Tammy illustrate the main thrust of this book: there is much to learn from the experiences of students as they prepare for and take their teacher licensure exams. As such, this book is made up of the experiences of students as they prepared for and took their teacher licensure exams. Some of these students passed the first time they took the exam; others passed after failing. And yet some others, like Tammy, ended up changing their majors because they did not pass the exam. What we have to learn from students in each of these categories is not a one-size-fits-all study plan or list of test-taking tips. Rather, we can learn how people came to understand what works for them and how they pushed through emotions like nervousness and anxiety. We can learn how people used the resources and people around them differently. We can learn how people dealt with ideas about cultural bias on exams and, yes, how some of them passed the exam and became teachers. These are essential insights for preservice teachers who are preparing to take their licensure exams.

Although this book is much different from test prep manuals, you might find some of those books useful alongside this one – especially if you are unfamiliar with the contents, format, or parameters of the particular exams your state requires you to take. It is unwise to walk into an exam without an idea about these aspects. Test prep manuals alone, however, will not unpack the human side of test preparation and execution from people whose experiences are similar to yours. That is where this book comes in and what it is about. Although this book is written directly for preservice teachers, faculty members in teacher education programs will benefit from it as well. It will give them insights into what preservice teachers experience as they prepare for their licensure exam as well as ideas about how to support them through this process.

Four Big Ideas

There are four big ideas running through this book that I should introduce now. The chapters in this book will give these ideas further attention, but a brief introduction to them now will prepare you to go more in depth later. The first of these ideas is thinking about the licensure exam as a collective rather than individual process. Most often, we think about tests and exams – especially high-stakes ones – as an individual pursuit, as something you do alone. There are good reasons to think about them as such. After all, few of us have ever taken an exam collectively or as a group. We may study in groups from time to time in preparation, but when the door shuts and you can "open your test booklet now," it's all you. The chapters in this book will challenge this solitary, individual interpretation of high-stakes exams. Your preparation for an exam takes place within a kind of social network – not a social network like Facebook but a network of ideas, people, and resources. A web, if you will. You hear about the exam and its level of difficulty from other people. They say, "Oh, it was easy!" Or, "It's hard! I heard nobody passed it!" Hearing about other people's experiences subtly shapes the ways we think about ourselves and our abilities. If I imagine a classmate of mine to be about as talented as I am, and they struggle with an exam, that tells me something about myself, vicariously so. Our ideas about ourselves are formed in context with this network of people around us. The purpose of thinking about the exam as a collective rather than individual process is to understand how we can use this collective network around us to our advantage.

Another big idea that runs through this book is paying attention to both the cognitive and affective aspects of licensure exam preparation. By cognitive, I am referring mostly to functions such as thinking, memory, reasoning, and the like that go into demonstrating knowledge that licensure exams are designed to test. When we think about licensure exams, we typically think about this cognitive realm: what you are supposed to know and demonstrate. But it is also important to consider the affective aspect of exam preparation. By the affective, I am referring to how emotions and feelings also factor into preparing for and taking your licensure exam. You likely feel different ways about your licensure exam. You might be nervous, excited, or something between these two different emotions. Or more subtly, we might say you have an affective disposition toward it that is less intense than a clear emotional feeling but definitely a *lean* toward or against it nonetheless. This lean can show itself in a number of different ways. Leaning away from the exam, you find yourself easily distracted from studying or preparing, as if even the slightest opportunity to do something else pushes you off your preparation course. Everything seems uphill. Leaning toward the exam is a much different experience. While you're not looking forward to the exam as if it is New Year's Eve, your forward lean presses you through the barriers in your path. You push through them as if they are thin like paper rather than thick like bricks. The contents of this book encourage you to think about both the cognitive and affective aspects of exam preparation, and the interaction between these two realms.

A third big idea through these chapters is developing a critical filter based upon your needs as an individual. As I've already noted in this chapter, I'm skeptical of one-size-fits-all approaches to test preparation. This skepticism is based on a simple principle but also upon my years of working closely with students preparing for their licensure exams. People have different needs, so what it takes to fulfil their needs is also different. Consequently, this book should push you to refine an understanding of your specific needs and filter out information that is not relevant to you. This ability becomes even more important when pressure increases. In high-pressure situations, oftentimes people latch onto any and all advice given to them. They'll try anything in hopes that it will work, even if it will get them just one more point. With this impulse, people spread themselves thin rather than arming themselves with a few specific approaches tethered to their needs. The most successful students in this book developed a critical filter for their preparation based upon their specific needs, and you should do the same though this book as you learn from their experiences.

A final big idea is attending to how social ideas about who you are, play into the licensure exam experience. I can illustrate this idea by sharing a personal story from graduate school that I haven't shared with many people. In graduate school, students typically have to complete what are called comprehensive or qualifying exams before they begin their dissertation. There are different ways that programs arrange and administer these exams, but they typically require knowledge from across the courses that graduate students have taken up until that point. In many instances, if you don't pass the exam, you're not allowed to proceed to the next stage of the program. The stakes tend to be very, very high.

One portion of my comprehensive exam took place in a two-hour timed session at a computer cubicle. We were given three things: a set of data, a research question, and a statistical analysis program on the computer. The task was to input the data into the program correctly, decipher what kind of statistical analysis should be run, properly run the analysis, and write up a discussion of the results. All alone. No notes. The clock ticking.

I began the task just as I had trained with my classmates over the past month. I opened up the program on the computer and started entering the numbers into the spreadsheet boxes. I was cruising and had the data carefully lined up after only about ten minutes. I reread the research question to double check the analysis procedure I was about to run. I had run these dozens of times in class and while practicing with my classmates. In fact, I was often the one explaining which procedure to run and telling my classmates that we'd all do fine on this exam. I deciphered the procedure like a skilled explorer reading a map: an independent sample t-test was what it called for. A couple clicks, a few options deep in the pulldown menu, and I was running my t-test. I'd probably finish with a half-hour to spare.

Except something went wrong. When the program finished running, the number output was a mess. It wasn't the neat number I expected or the kind of number that comes when you properly run the procedure. It was something indecipherable. Something was wrong – very wrong.

Instead of working through what went wrong, I was immobilized in these moments by a flood of memories from over the course of my graduate program. These weren't random memories. They were memories connected by one aspect of who I was or how other people saw me: my age. I was the youngest person in my graduate cohort. This age difference among my classmates and me most often played out along the lines of what we did outside of class. I went surfing the mornings before class and worked as a DJ at clubs in the evenings – not typical graduate school stuff, at least not for the people in my program. These characteristics were not lost on the people around me. Occasionally, my classmates would make sense of my age and presence in a graduate program by assuming that I must somehow be very gifted. (My 2.98 undergraduate GPA suggests that I most certainly was not.) These assumptions came across in subtle, well-intended comments. I knew the assumptions weren't true, but they lingered with me.

Staring at my computer screen, I wasn't frozen. I was pinned down, feeling the weight of all these comments and interactions over the years stacking up on top of me. Under this weight, my mind raced and thought about what a surprise and epic failure it would seem to everyone if I failed the exam. *Me.* Who they thought I was – even though I knew it not to be true – would be burst, shattered. Scenes started to play out in my head as I tried to regroup: what they would say when word got around that I failed, how they would react, what my advisor would think. The numbers in front of me made even less sense with this anxiety growing inside of me. Gathering myself, I decided to start over. I closed the windows on my computer and restarted the program. Mentally, I tried to do the same with the last 30 minutes of my life sitting in that room: erase them and start over. When I went through the steps for the second time (and entered the data into the program correctly!), the results turned out as expected.

How I made it through the challenge is not the important part here. What's important is recognizing that in these moments of struggle and anxiety, who I was – or who I felt other people believed me to be, the identities they put on me – shaped the ways I experienced the high-pressure situation. In this situation, it was my age and how much younger my classmates perceived me to be. For other people in different situations, it might be gender, race and ethnicity, or something else. This is the final big idea I'll take-up in the pages that follow: how social ideas about who you are play into the licensure exam experience and what to do about it.

Where This Book Came From

There is much variation among states with regard to which licensure exam they use, when preservice teachers have to take the exams, and what cut-off scores they must meet. Some states use exams created by Educational Testing Service; others use exams made by Pearson. In some teacher education programs, students must pass a professional readiness exam (sometimes called a "basic skills" test) before they can be admitted. Some states allow students to substitute SAT or ACT scores for one of these exams. Much of this action happens at the undergraduate level, but in some states like California where certification is entirely post-baccalaureate, the exams happen elsewhere. Content area exams tied to specific areas of teaching – elementary education and secondary content areas – have different schedules as well. Some programs require students to pass these before proceeding onto certain courses, and others simply require passing the exam before recommending students for licensure. If this variation isn't confusing enough, sometime states change the exams they are using without too much notice to the people who have to take them. Performance exams like edTPA are a different beast that I won't get into here.

The insights in this book come from the experiences of preservice teachers studying to take a professional readiness exam required for admission into their undergraduate teacher education program. Most of them also took content area exams before completing the capstone teaching internship, but this book comes from their experiences specifically with the Praxis I professional readiness exam created and administered by Educational Testing Service. (You will hear students sometimes refer to this exam simply by calling it "Praxis.") Since this book is not a study guide for a specific exam or content, readers taking other licensure exams and in different configurations will still find valuable takeaways.

Some preservice teachers in this book passed the exam on their first try without studying much at all. Others studied, prepared themselves diligently, and passed. And yet others studied, prepared themselves diligently, and did not pass. Some students passed after multiple tries, and yet some ultimately decided it was best if they stopped trying to pass the exam and changed majors instead. For some very capable preservice teachers, the exam score was one of the few barriers that kept them from success in a teacher education program. For others, the exam score was a signal of more troubles to come if they would have continued further into the program. In all, the main insights in this book come from students who had a range of experiences and levels of success on their licensure exam. We have something to learn from students at each point along this range.

This book, however, is not these students simply giving you advice about how to prepare yourself for an exam. You could get advice like this from people around you. Throughout the book, I analyze these students' experiences and present the insights that we can learn from them. At times, I also step outside of these students' experiences and summarize some of the results from important academic studies that can give you a different view of licensure exams and yourself as a test-taker. Studies like these often appear in stuffy academic journals filled with jargon, so I take care to talk about these studies in straightforward and plain language that is relevant to you.

While completing this book, I occasionally received emails from test preparation and tutoring companies advertising their services. In most instances, these companies would guarantee the success of their programs: that 90% of people who participated ended up passing whatever exam they needed to take. In their ads, these companies sometimes used language to suggest they had "cracked the code" and "figured out the test." These claims and guarantees often struck me as overly simplistic. How could they crack the code of tests that are often changing? Or what about the tests where the required passing score varied by state? Most of all, how can a one-size-fits-all approach work for people who are so different from one another? My experience suggests to me that guarantees and platitudes like these – although they are easy to latch onto in times of desperate need – oversimplify the process. Consequently, I stop short at the outset of this book from guaranteeing that if you read and apply it, you'll pass whatever exam you are preparing for. Things aren't that simple. Instead of guaranteeing success, I am more confident guaranteeing growth. From the successes and struggles of students in this book, you will grow into a deeper understanding of yourself as a test-taker, learner, and future educator.

Overview of Chapters and Application Activities

The chapters in this book are divided into three parts. I direct the contents of the first two parts toward preservice teachers. As such, each of the chapters in these two parts is followed by a series of application and extension activities that generate from its chapter contents. In Part 1, "Rethinking Struggle and Support," chapters drill down into some of the challenges that students experience with taking licensure exams and some of the unexpected forms of support.

Chapter 2 addresses one of the most widespread beliefs about high-stakes exams: that some people are just born good test-takers. The chapter addresses this belief by focusing on three in-depth cases of students who passed their licensure exam after multiple failed attempts. Shonda, who you met earlier, is one of these students. This chapter focuses on the changes in preparation that these students made between failing and passing the exam, such as how they addressed their weaknesses, strategized for optimal test space and time, and paid attention to (and sometimes blocked out) the social messages around them. The application and extension that follows this chapter focuses on how you see yourself in comparison to the three case studies and an evaluation of yourself by way of the main themes in the chapter.

Chapter 3 addresses the idea that preparing for and taking a licensure exam is a collective rather than individual process. The chapter demonstrates how thoughtful preparation takes place within a network of different people, ideas, and resources. I map out – both visually and narratively – the preparation networks of four students as the basis for this chapter. These four cases help us to understand the different ways that preparation networks can support or hinder success. The application and extension for this chapter leads you through some exercises to map out, understand, and create your own preparation network by identifying key people and resources around you.

Part 2, "Addressing What's Felt but Not Seen," deals with aspects of teacher licensure exams that are easy to miss but crucial nonetheless. Chapter 4 addresses a common idea that is associated with standardized tests: that they are culturally biased against particular student groups. Most often, people hold this idea with respect to students of color, but it can also pertain to adult students, rural students, or students from low-income backgrounds. This chapter demystifies the notion of cultural bias in standardized tests and reframes it in an honest and useful way. This knowledge will keep you from believing simplistic rumors about the exam. I illustrate some of the healthy and harmful ways students have dealt with ideas of bias while preparing for and taking licensure exams. The application and extension that follows this chapter leads you through the important work of excavating your own beliefs about standardized tests and bias, understanding where they came from, and reframing them in productive ways.

Chapter 5 addresses the emotions and affective states that play into test preparation and performance. Addressing emotions and affective states is important because they can inhibit or facilitate working memory, executive functions, and other processes that are necessary to perform well. This chapter covers this topic by focusing on the different ways that students cope with stress associated with licensure exams and the personal narratives they build around that stress. The application and extension from this chapter picks up on these two ideas. They help you to understand how you cope with stress associated with the exam, the positive and negative result of this coping, and how you narrate these experiences.

Although this book is written directly to preservice teachers, faculty members in teacher education programs have a great deal to learn from it as well. I direct Part 3, "How Faculty Members Can Support Preservice Teachers," to this latter group. Chapter 6 unpacks how to view licensure exams and students' experiences with them through two frameworks and related concepts: self-efficacy and sociocultural theory. I also attend in this chapter to the screening and signaling function of licensure exams. I argue that teacher educators should make program policies and actions based upon an understanding of these functions, rather than leave preservice teachers to fend for themselves. In Chapter 7, I turn toward specific recommendations for how teacher educators can support their preservice teachers toward success on licensure exams. I draw from the two frameworks and related concepts of Chapter 6 to outline these recommendations for program and classroom levels. Overall, this chapter provides faculty members with practical takeaways so that they build students up to admission into the teacher education program rather than screen them out through licensure exams.

An Inch Wide and a Mile Deep

2

How Students Pass After Failing the First Time

One of the most common beliefs about standardized tests is that some people are simply good at taking them and other people are not. According to this belief, a certain segment of the population is able to work well under pressure, speed through different kinds of problems, and make good multiple choice guesses – all due to luck of the genetic lottery. They are simply born with it. Other people are on the losing side of the lottery: they're just not good at these tests, and they will continue to perform poorly. If you've ever struggled with a standardized test, you've likely wondered about this idea.

At the outset of this chapter, my goal is not to dismiss this possibility outright. If you hold this belief at all, it is probably related to some experiences you've had. This is how ideas, experiences, and beliefs often work: an idea shapes how you interpret your experiences, and this gives way to a belief. Continued experiences and the belief then reinforce and sustain one another. Consequently, you are unlikely to change your mind simply because someone like me tells you a belief is not true. Instead, before we get into some specific cases from students, I'd like us to take a deeper look at the belief that some people are born good standardized test-takers and others are not.

First, what exactly do we mean by the claim that some people are good at taking standardized tests? To get some clarity, we should unpack the specific skills that are implied in the quality of "good standardized test-taker." This description typically means three things. First, since virtually all standardized tests are timed, it means that a person can work well in timed situations, accessing and demonstrating what they know. Working well in a timed situation means that a person can handle pressure. They are able to take tasks one step at a time and not get too rattled or anxious when something doesn't go their way. So, we should connect working in a timed situation with handling pressure. Second, being a good standardized test-taker implies that a person functions well in a new, foreign environment. Most high-stakes standardized exams take place in an environment that is unfamiliar. It may be an official test center with rows of computer cubicles or an education institution that is a host site for an exam on a Saturday morning. Either way, people often have to experience a new and unfamiliar environment and demonstrate their knowledge in this context. Finally, being a good standardized test-taker often means someone can work at their best ability early in the morning. Although it is becoming more common for people to take exams in the afternoon at test centers, more often than not, taking an exam means doing so early in the morning when few people are at their highest functioning capacity.

Consequently, when we think of someone who is a good at taking standardized tests, we should realize this means handling three things: time-pressured situations, unfamiliar environments, and early mornings. No more, no less.

I want you to keep these ideas in mind as we turn toward an important research study about test-takers who struggled to pass their professional readiness exam.[1] The research team led by Drew Gitomer at Educational Testing Service (the company that makes the Praxis exam) addressed a question that has probably crossed your mind at some point too: whether or not professional readiness exams are unnecessary obstacles on your way to becoming a teacher. Also implied within this question is if the exams reveal useful information about how well someone might perform later in a teacher education program, or even into their career in the classroom. The research team tested this idea by looking at students who had to take a professional readiness exam early in their teacher education program and then a content area exam later. The researchers compared how three groups of test-takers performed on their content area licensure exam (e.g., elementary education, secondary education subject areas, etc.). Here are the three groups the researchers were interested in:

- Students who passed their professional readiness exam the first time they took it.
- Students who passed the exam after more than one attempt.
- Students who never passed it.

The researchers called these last two groups the "borderline group" because they were on the threshold or border of passing. The researchers were interested in finding out if there were any differences among these groups with their performance on *content area* exams. If these groups performed similarly on content area exams, then the earlier professional readiness exam they took previously would seem to be an unnecessary obstacle. Why require students to take this gatekeeping exam that could keep them out of a teacher education program if they similarly passed their content area exam? But if there were key differences between the groups on content area exams, then the professional readiness exam might be telling something important about these students' abilities – specifically, that they lacked important skills that would be necessary later in the program. The researchers were interested in other variables too, but the questions about the borderline group shed important light on whether people are simply born to be good standardized test-takers or not.

The results of the study were somewhat anticlimactic: they showed that the more people struggle with professional readiness exams, the more they struggle with content area exams later on. The inverse was also true: the less people struggle with professional readiness exams, the less they struggle with content area exams later on. Of course, there were exceptions to each of these trends, but the general results suggested that the professional readiness exam was a useful signal about who would pass the content area exam later on. Perhaps results like these are not surprising from researchers working at a test company.

You might look at the result of the study as confirming some common assumptions about standardized test-taking ability. "See, I was right!" you might say. "Students who struggled continued to fail, and students who did well continued to do so. You either know it or you don't." In that case, the only option is to close this book now and forget about passing if you've already struggled. You'd be wrong to do that because you haven't met Shonda, Heather, and Destiny.

Shonda, Heather, and Destiny were students of mine in a teacher education program. I had each of them in class and worked alongside them during field internships, campus events, and education service projects over the four years they were in college. They had a number of things in common: each was a committed, hard-working, African American, elementary education major with a passion for educational justice. Each of them also failed their professional readiness exam the first time they took it, sometimes failing multiple times. Yet, eventually, each of them went on to pass not only the professional readiness exam but the content area exam too. Each of them graduated as a licensed teacher. If we think about the borderline group from the study above, each of the women fit that description since they struggled to pass the professional readiness exam. But, their success cuts against the trend in the study. Despite struggling with the exam, each went on to be successful and enter the classroom as a licensed teacher. What kinds of things did they do between failing and passing the exam? What changes in test preparation, thinking, and other areas did they make? How did they "become" good standardized test-takers? Let's find out.

What They Were Up Against

There are a few details about the exam and scoring of it that play into students' experiences below. Shonda, Heather, and Destiny took a professional readiness exam that was offered on paper-and-pencil format early in the morning or on a computerized format by individual appointment at a testing center. Like most professional readiness exams, it consisted of three separate, timed tests of reading, writing, and math. The tests could be taken together in one exam administration or in separate administrations. The paper version of the exam was offered four times a year. The test company sent scores to test-takers about four to six weeks after the exam. Computer-based administrations were available more frequently because students could simply make an appointment with a test company at a date and time of their choice, though this format was more expensive than the paper-based test. Students could see their scores on the computer-based exam right after finishing it (except for the written essay score). These different formats and timeframes meant that students had some different options available to them.

There is a wide range of score configurations on licensure exams. These configurations depend on the particular exam a person is taking and the state in which they are taking it. For the exam Shonda, Heather, and Destiny took, the possible scores on each test ranged from 150 to 190. How is that for confusing? During the time these students took the exam, their state permitted two methods of passing. Most directly, test-takers could meet or surpass the passing score on each test (reading: 172; writing: 173; math: 173), or they could pass by meeting a composite score of 521. The composite score method means that a test-taker's strength in an area could help compensate for a weakness in a different area. There was one catch with the composite score, however. To pass by this method, test-takers had to meet a *minimum* required score on each exam (reading: 169;

writing: 170; math: 170). This minimum score requirement meant that students could not score too low in any one area. Test-takers did not need to choose or designate one of these two methods of passing. They typically took all of the tests to see if they could receive individual passing scores. If they did not receive the necessary scores, the composite score method provided them with an additional avenue to strategize for success. While some of these details may be confusing, they factor into the students' situations below.

Shonda: "You Know You Can Do It ... So Get It Together"

Shonda took all three of the exams in one sitting the spring of her sophomore year. She looked briefly at a test preparation booklet before taking the exams but, by her own admittance, did not study much. Describing herself as "not a standardized test person in general," she recalled all of the drill-and-kill standardized test preparation she experienced in high school: "It was too much for me, doing the test [preparation] over and over. By the time I got to the real test, I didn't care anymore. I practiced so much on my own, I'd get to the real thing and mentally I'd be over it." Trying to avoid this cycle with the professional readiness exam, she went in without much preparation. She passed the reading and writing exams in this initial sitting but did not pass the math. She was a whopping eleven points short. To put this gap in perspective, there were 40 questions on the math test. If each question was worth one point, the score margin she needed to improve was equivalent to about one-quarter of the test. That was a lot.

Two months later as the summer was starting, Shonda sat for the math exam once again but elected to take the computerized version rather than the paper version she had taken in the spring. Like before, she did not prepare much. She "hoped for the best and thought maybe it would be different," perhaps because she was taking the computerized format and not the paper format like the first time. It wasn't. She received the same score she had three months earlier and was still eleven points from passing. At least she was consistent!

In the fall when Shonda returned to campus, she pushed back against her resistance to prepare by taking specific steps to pass the math exam. The teacher education department paired her up with Patrice, a secondary education mathematics major who had passed the same exam on her first attempt and with very high scores. Patrice's approach for helping Shonda was to diagnose two or three specific math skills on the exam that Shonda had not mastered, such as probability and statistics. They concentrated not only on mastering those skills but also on identifying the different problem types through which those skills would appear on the exam. If Shonda could master those skills and identify those problems, they figured, she would correctly answer these kinds of problems on the exam. This approach meant deciding not to focus on all of the math content covered on the exam. Meeting together once a week, they used many of the same resources that Shonda had only glanced at before she took the exam the first time. Patrice brought in additional resources targeted toward these areas, and Shonda eventually sought out resources as well after she learned to identify the relevant problem types. Patrice also gave Shonda specific tactics to approach the exam when she took it for the third time. She advised Shonda that when the exam period began, she should first identify all of the questions that were the types they had worked on and to complete these questions first. This way Shonda's score was sure to reflect her newly acquired skills; she wouldn't miss any of these questions if, for example, they were placed at the end of the exam and she ran out of time. Patrice also told Shonda to skip problems that would take too long to compute or problems that she didn't know and to come back to these at the end of the exam. This tactic would ensure that Shonda's time was spent on the questions she was most likely to get right.

Who Shonda was speaking to and what they told her was also part of this process. Shonda frequently spoke with her mother and grandmother about the exam after she took it the first two times and as she prepared for the third try. The way they made sense of her initial failures helped frame her thinking. They reminded Shonda that she hadn't done anything to prepare the first two times, and that this is why she failed. She narrated her internal monologue, shaped by her mother and grandmother:

> For the most part, it was just, *okay, Shonda, you know what you need to do to pass the test. You know you can do it. You didn't do anything before to pass it. So get it together....This is the third time, get it together. You know what you need to do.*

When Shonda took the math exam for the third time that fall, she was even more anxious than before because she needed to pass the exam in order to be admitted into upper division courses in her teacher education program, lest she have to change her major. When the exam period began, she proceeded through the exam according the plan Patrice had given her, first identifying and completing the question types they had worked on and then prioritizing the questions she judged to be easiest. When she finished taking the exam, she did not have a strong sense that she passed. In fact, taking the exam felt very similar to the previous times she had taken it. When her score arrived in the mail roughly a month later, it had increased thirteen points, exceeding the cutoff requirement by two points.

In the following semesters, Shonda went on to complete her capstone student teaching internship, pass her content area exams, and receive her teaching license. She claimed that her experience with the professional readiness exam didn't change her perspective on herself or her abilities: "I knew I could do it before, I just didn't apply myself. And I already knew if I didn't apply myself, I'm not going to get the results that I know I can get." Similarly, her experience did not change her perspective on high-stakes standardized exams, or the anxiousness and fatigue she associates with them. "I know that if I apply myself I can deal with it, but that anxiety still hasn't changed for me."

Heather: "I Used All the Tools in My Toolbox"

Heather took all three exams in the paper-based format in one sitting the summer before her sophomore year. Like Shonda, she did not prepare much for the exams this first time around. She held a fixed belief about standardized test-taking ability, thinking that they were configured in such a way that studying for them could not help much. "My philosophy was, you either know it or you don't," she remarked. Heather passed the writing exam, which was not a surprise to her since, in her own estimation, writing and language arts have always come easy to her. She fell one point short of passing the reading exam and eleven points short on the mathematics exam. This low score on mathematics was not a surprise to her because she considered it her weakest area.

When Heather returned to campus in the fall, she found that many of the classmates around her had passed the exam. She would occasionally ask other people in the program how they did on the exam and wish them congratulations if they passed, but she intentionally stopped short of asking them for advice or direction. She justified this decision by stating, "I know that I have a different thought process. I know that my strengths are different than their strengths and my weaknesses are different than their weaknesses." In preparation to retake the math exam that fall, she took actions that challenged her belief that "You either know it or you don't." She used a preparation booklet with sample problems and sought tutoring targeted toward her weaknesses from a math education professor in the department. She also had a mathematics education course that fall taught by the same professor. This tutoring and instruction from the professor was important to Heather because she felt she could not teach herself math. Unlike Shonda's, however, this tutoring did not include specific strategies to approach the exam, like prioritizing easier math questions and skimming reading passages before answering questions. Heather was already aware of these strategies and had used them in her previous exam sitting. Her preparation for the reading exam remained minimal since she only needed one more point to pass and considered herself strong in language arts.

In this second sitting, her math score increased seven points, a tremendous accomplishment. But it was still four points short of passing. Her reading score increased one point and met the cutoff score exactly. The next fall, with another mathematics education course under her belt, she took the math exam for a third time and scored two points higher. This new score was still two points short of passing, but it met the minimum state required score, thus making her eligible to pass the exam through a composite score if her total on all three exams reached 521.

Instead of retaking the mathematics exam for a fourth time, Heather returned to her strength: reading. She decided to retake the reading exam and shoot for a higher score even though she had already passed it. If she could score two points higher than her previous passing score, she would meet the composite score and pass the test without having to pass the math portion outright. This time she prepared for the reading exam by printing out some review materials from the test company and making an appointment at a computerized testing center to take the exam at noon, a change from all of the early mornings she had taken the paper-based exam before. Instead of studying the night before like she had in the past, she relaxed by putting herself through some writing exercises I had recommended that focused on the values that are important to her – not the exam. During the exam the next day, Heather made a deliberate effort to pace herself through the session and leave time to review her answers at the end. She identified that this new strategy came from a conversation she had with me. When Heather received her score at the end of the session, it was eight points higher than in her previous sitting. With a composite score of 527, she had passed the professional readiness exam without having to take the math exam a fourth time.

Thinking about her journey to pass, she summarized: "I think overall, it was the combination of all the tools that were in my toolbox." With this statement, she referred to the instruction and tutoring from her math education professor, the advice from me, the study materials, and taking the exam in the afternoon rather than the morning. This final point was particularly important. She emphasized that taking the exam at a time that coordinated with her biorhythms was an incredibly important factor in her score jump. Instead of waking up at 6:00 a.m. to take a morning exam on an empty stomach, the individual appointment at the computerized testing center allowed her to wake up at a more normal time, eat, study that morning, pray, and pace herself throughout the morning leading up to the exam in the afternoon.

Like Shonda, Heather reported that all along she thought she had the skills to pass the exam. Consequently, her success did not radically change perceptions about her skills or abilities. Upon this success, however, she reported feeling less nervous and more confident with regard to the elementary education content area exam she would take later in the program. She also felt the experience prepared her to help her own students in the future who might have similar experiences with high-stakes standardized exams. In the subsequent semesters, Heather went on to complete her capstone student teaching experience and pass the necessary content area exam (exceeding the passing score by fifteen points) to be licensed to teach in her home state of Maryland.

Destiny: "I'm Glad This Happened, Honestly. It Wasn't a Waste of Time"

Destiny took a different approach to the exams than the other students. She started with what she felt was her strongest area, mathematics, and took that exam first, separate from the other exams during her sophomore year. She passed, exceeding the cutoff score by four points. The next semester, she took the reading and writing exams without much preparation and did not pass them. She needed three more points to pass the writing exam, and a steep ten more points to pass the reading. As she did with math, she decided to split up the reading and writing tests moving forward.

She prepared intensely to retake the writing exam but focused only on the timed essay portion and not on the multiple choice questions about grammar and writing conventions. Since the essay counted for half of the entire writing exam score, she felt it was best to focus her energy there instead of spreading it thin across esoteric grammar topics. Destiny was an excellent writer, but she was an iterative and nonlinear writer. She normally spent time writing, revising, and rewriting to refine her essays for courses. Because of this approach, time – not grammar or argumentation – was her main concern. In order to cut down the time it would take her to write under pressure, she looked at all 71 of the sample essay prompts provided on the test overview and outlined a response to every single one of them. She also attended the weekly study session for the exam and wrote practice essays under time constraints to some prompts and received feedback from me. This meticulous preparation took much time and energy, particularly mid-semester when midterm exams, scholarship applications, and other campus obligations intensified. Yet, she felt this approach would save her valuable time during the exam.

During this period of preparation, Destiny was intentional about how and with whom she talked about the exam. She referenced "definitely not talking about it" in class and in social settings when other students might be commiserating about the exam, talking about how difficult they felt it was, or trying to devise a way of progressing through the major without passing the exam. "I definitely kept my feelings to myself when everyone was talking about, *Oh, was it easy? Was it hard?*" A critical aspect of avoiding these conversations for her was *identifying* that these conversations were negative and not productive for her. Many of the conversations did not seem negative at first; they were just groups of students talking about their experiences with program requirements. "It don't seem negative when you're talking about it," she summarized. "You just have to really identify it." She avoided conversations with students who were complaining or talking negatively about the exam.

Destiny did talk about the exam among a close circle of supportive friends. Some of these friends were other students diligently preparing – "People that was serious about it and telling me that I can do this and not people that was saying, *Oh my god, it's so hard!*" While talking with these people, she paid attention to the tone she used. "I wouldn't talk about it like, *Ugh! The exam, it's annoying! Ugh!* Like that. I didn't want to think about it like that. I wanted to think about it as, *You can do this.* I didn't want to think about the negative and negativity behind it." She also latched onto one critical message from an unlikely source. Destiny had a passing conversation with Megan one day after class. A classmate with whom Destiny wasn't particularly close, Megan had passed the exam with high scores on her first attempt. "One thing that really stuck with me," Destiny remembered, "She said, *Destiny, it's not that bad. You can do this.* That stuck with me to this day." Destiny even remembered the exact room where Megan said this to her.

When Destiny retook the writing portion of the exam, her deep preparation for the essay paid off. The prompt was one she had written a practice essay for. Like the other time she took the writing exam, she wrote, scribbled, and erased right up until the time limit. A few weeks later she received her new score that was two points higher than her last sitting. This score was one point below passing but met the state minimum score, thus making her eligible to pass the exam through the composite score method if all of her scores totaled 521.

Before Destiny retook the reading exam, she checked out two practice books from the university library and did practice problems in them about every other day. Unlike when she retook the writing exam during the busy semester, she retook the reading exam over winter break in her hometown of Brooklyn, New York City. She made a personal appointment at a computerized testing center. She found this environment "very intense" compared to the paper exam settings held at neighboring universities. The security procedures included showing IDs and having her photo taken, locking all personal items in a locker, being searched with a metal detector, and having security cameras on her while taking the exam. The test center was also on the 14th floor of a building directly across from a New York City Board of Education Building, which she found added extra intimidation and a bit of irony. While retaking the test, Destiny committed to "immediately choose an answer that I thought could possibly be remotely right" for the questions that were more complex or would take more energy. She then marked these questions and revisited and reworked them at the end of the exam with the remaining time. Specifically on the reading exam during this sitting, she skipped long or boring reading passages in favor of completing shorter or more interesting passages first. Destiny came up with the strategies on her own after realizing that for her, the challenge of the exam was not about knowledge or skill. She had those. The challenge was racing against the clock. She then asked herself, "Out of all the test-taking strategies out there, which one would most benefit my situation?" and then selected strategies that would help save her time.

Since she took the computerized format of the exam this time, she received her score at the test center right after finishing it. She had scored twelve points higher than her previous sitting and surpassed the reading exam cutoff score by two points. Not only had she passed the reading exam, her new score bumped her composite score above the 521-point threshold for passing. This meant she did not have to retake her writing exam another time to score one more point or execute any of her other backup plans. She had passed the professional readiness requirement by composite score. She was finished. Like Shonda, Destiny did not have a strong sense that she passed in this sitting. This sense was related to the intense and intimidating environment of the computerized testing center. "I couldn't believe I passed so high being under surveillance every move I made," she noted. "It was just really intimidating. I couldn't believe that I did so well." She also felt that the fewer obligations and no distractions between semesters played a large role in freeing her up to study and pass.

Passing the exam turned out to be the first real concrete goal of her college career. She described her approach before the exam as passive, simply taking opportunities as they came her way. "Now I'm constantly making goals for myself and trying my best to achieve them," she stated, such as passing the elementary education content area exam, going to graduate school, and getting scholarships. She meant this statement about concrete goals beyond her major as well. After passing the professional readiness exam, she made two big goals and accomplished both of them: to study abroad over the summer and enroll in a demanding summer intensive immersion course. "I'm glad this happened, honestly. It wasn't a waste of time." She began the next semester enthusiastic about preparing for the elementary education content area exam, asking professors in the department for the study books before semester courses even started. Like the others, she went on to complete her student teaching internship, pass her final licensure exam, and secure a teaching job. She looked back on the experience as an "eye opener" that prepared her for real demands that await her in the profession.

Looking Across These Experiences

These students' experiences reveal something important about preparing for and passing a licensure exam. However, there are additional insights if we take some time and look across these students' experiences for certain threads. There are four threads we'll examine, specifically: 1) targeted and proactive preparation, 2) unconventional strategies and test wiseness, 3) optimal test space and time, and 4) intentionality in social circles and messages.

An Inch Wide and a Mile Deep: Targeted and Proactive Preparation

Shonda, Heather, and Destiny prepared minimally before taking the exam the first time yet prepared diligently for the times they retook the exam. In preparation for retakes, they focused on a specific area or areas of an exam where they had the most opportunity to make up points, rather than spreading themselves thin by studying all of the content covered in the exam. In this way, their preparation was an inch wide and a mile deep. They also located new test preparation material or utilized test preparation material that they already had in new ways. This kind of preparation was different from simply focusing on areas of weakness, a more conventional approach to preparation. Mastering an area that did not have many points attached to it on the exam would not lead to a significant score increase. An area of weakness was only worth focusing on if there were substantial points attached to it. Additionally, as was the case with Heather and Destiny, they leveraged their strengths in order to garner more points in addition to or instead of focusing solely on their weaknesses.

Targeted preparation for some students required acting against some of the beliefs they held about the exam and their potential on it. Think back to Heather's perspective on the exam and her abilities. She believed "you either know it or you don't" and that there wasn't much she could do to prepare for it, especially on her own. Even though Heather expressed this belief, she took actions against it. She located and used new study materials, sought tutoring from a math professor, and more. Do these actions mean that she actually believed something different about standardized test-taking ability? It's hard to say. Often people's actions are not in line with their beliefs, and in Heather's case, that seems to be a good thing. Similarly with Shonda, she resisted preparing for the exam at first due to test-preparation fatigue that lingered from high school. She pushed back against this resistance in order to engage in targeted preparation with Patrice.

More than Studying: Unconventional Strategies and Test Wiseness

The experiences of the students in this chapter also point to the ways that unconventional strategies and test wiseness can factor into passing the exam. Test wiseness is a concept that is often overlooked today but can be traced back to the 1960s. Jason Millman and colleagues described it as a person's "capacity to utilize the characteristics and formats of the test and/ or the test-taking situation to receive a high score."[2] What they mean here is that there are insights and tactics that a person can use from the exam itself in order to do better. If you've ever eliminated an answer option on a multiple choice test and then made an educated guess from the remaining options, you've used a basic idea from test wiseness. You used the multiple choice format of the test to help increase your chances of getting a question correct. Millman and colleagues argued that there are independent and dependent test wiseness strategies. Independent strategies are independent of the subject matter the test items are designed to measure. These kinds of strategies are intended to save time, guess with higher probability of correctness, avoid errors, and reason deductively. Dependent strategies, as the name suggests, are dependent on the construction and purpose of the test. These kind of strategies include recognizing specific words and idiosyncrasies in the test that help distinguish correct and incorrect answers.[3] Some of the advice you read in test prep manuals is rooted in test wiseness. To be clear, test wiseness tactics are *not* substitutes for knowing the material that a test is designed to cover. They're not magic. Rather, they work in tandem with this knowledge.

Similar to test wiseness strategies are unconventional strategies. These are solutions that rely on insight, logic, or estimation and are typically not taught in textbooks.[4] Unconventional strategies are often useful on standardized math exams because they eliminate many of the computational steps a person would take to solve a problem – the kinds of steps we often learn in school. While this may seem counterintuitive, each computational step is a chance for you to make a mistake. Using estimation or insight reduces the chances you have to make a mistake, and they also save time. Table 2.1 illustrates a conventional and unconventional approach to a math problem.

In different degrees, each of the students used test wiseness or unconventional strategies during the retake administrations that they passed. In most cases, they noted that they did not use these strategies during the previous exam administrations, or they used them in lesser degrees. Most common among the participants were *time-use strategies* designed to reduce

Table 2.1   Conventional and Unconventional Strategies

Example:

Which of the following fractions is equal to .375?

A. ⅙
B. ½
C. ⅜
D. ¾

Conventional strategy: Convert the decimal into a fraction	*Unconventional strategy: Logic and estimation*
Put the decimal over 1 in a fraction: .375/1	Since the decimal is smaller than .5, the correct answer must be a fraction smaller than ½
Multiply the numerator by 1000, which is 375	Therefore, eliminate choices B and D
Multiply the denominator by 1000, which is 1000	⅜ (answer C) is closer to one-half than ⅙ (answer A) is, and .375 is also close to one-half (i.e., .5)
Put these numbers back into a fraction, which is $375/1000$	Therefore, the answer is likely answer C
Simply the fraction:	
Divide the numerator by 125, which is 3	
Divide the denominator by 125, which is 8	
Put these numbers into a fraction, which is ⅜	
The answer is ⅜	

Source: Adopted from Keena Arbuthnot, "The Effects of Stereotype Threat on Standardized Mathematics Test Performance and Cognitive Processing," *Harvard Education Review* 79, no. 3 (2009): 448–72.

the time required to answer questions, thus allowing them to get through all items and finish the exam.[5] These strategies looked different depending on the specific exam that participants were taking. For Destiny trying to finish the essay portion of the writing exam, this strategy meant outlining a response to each of the 71 possible essay prompts in the weeks prior to the exam. For Shonda and Heather on the math test, this strategy meant prioritizing questions that they knew or had prepared for and doing these questions first. On the reading exam, this strategy meant doing shorter or more interesting passages first and marking longer or more boring ones for consideration at the end. All of these strategies were intended to save them time or increase their chances of completing questions they had a higher probability of getting correct.

I need to be clear at this point that test wiseness and unconventional strategies were not tricks that alone helped the students to pass. Recall all of the targeted effort the women put in between failing and passing, and all of the content that they refreshed themselves on and learned. Test wiseness and unconventional strategies can be seductive because, improperly understood, they could lead us to believe there is an easy solution: "Do these tricks and you'll pass." A person with all the test wiseness in the world but little content knowledge related to the exam will most certainly fail. Shonda, Heather, and Destiny illustrate the proper understanding and use of test wiseness and unconventional strategies: they operate in tandem *with* devoted preparation and knowledge.

Making a Way: Strategizing for Optimal Test Space and Time

The students' experiences also reveal insights about how they strategized for different score options to pass the exam and sought out the test administration settings that would support them to get those scores. To recall, only Shonda passed the exam by meeting or exceeding the required scores on the reading, writing, and math tests. Heather and Destiny passed through the composite score method. This alternate method afforded them different avenues to strategize passing the exam, such as leveraging their strengths to cover for a weakness instead of taking a specific exam yet another time.

Each of the students utilized the computerized testing format because it gave them more control over an important factor working against them: time. The clock was ticking against them to pass the exam for admission into their teacher education program. Though more expensive, the computerized format kept them from losing time by waiting for a paper-based administration that happens only every three months. Receiving their score right away on the computer, they were able to strategize their next move immediately, rather than wait up to six weeks for the score from a paper-based exam. Furthermore, the students could retake the exam sooner in this computerized format, break it up into its individual tests across multiple retake sessions, and schedule it at a time of the semester (or between semesters) or a location that would be less stressful for them. Finally, the computerized format also put them in control of the time of day they took the exam. They no longer had to take the exam at 7:30 a.m., the absurdly early time of the paper-based exam. While time of day may seem like an insignificant factor related to success, recall that Heather pinpointed that taking the exam at a time of day aligned with her biorhythms was perhaps the most important factor to her reading score increasing twelve points.

Intentionality in Social Circles and Messages

Relationships with key people also played into how Shonda, Heather, and Destiny prepared to retake exams. Shonda had Patrice, her math tutor, who facilitated the preparation for her second retake. Patrice diagnosed Shonda's areas of weakness, located relevant resources, and gave her test wiseness strategies that she had not considered. Shonda spoke with her mother and grandmother about her preparation and latched onto key messages from them that shaped the positive way she made sense of her initial failure. Heather had her math education professor, who provided instruction and tutoring, and I provided her with advice and strategies as well. I worked extensively with Destiny as she prepared for the timed essay, and a lasting message from Megan, an acquaintance from class, seemed to boost her belief in her capabilities. Consequently, preparation was seldom an isolated activity for these students. They received resources, strategies, advice, and key messages from other people that factored into their success.

Among these relevant relationships, however, only Shonda's relationship with her mother and grandmother could be considered close and longstanding. The other relationships relevant to test preparation were temporary, situational, and not with close friends. Why is this? A long-standing principle of social network theory, "the strength of weak ties," helps explain.[6] The concept of "weak ties" refers to relationships with people or sources of information that are of shorter time duration, have less interpersonal connection, or low reciprocity. They are people you might not know very well or that come into your life for only a short period of time. Conversely, relationships with strong ties – like close friendships – are usually of longer duration, have high levels of interpersonal connection, and high reciprocity. We normally think of these strong ties as what we need to get us through difficult situations, and we do. But the strength of *weak ties* lies in their ability to provide new information to change practice, spur, innovate, and alter behavior – things that strong ties typically do not provide. This concept helps explain why it was more often weak relationships (like with Patrice and Megan), rather than strong ones with close friends, that provided students with new information and resources to help them pass.

Students were not open to all messages in their social circles, however. To recall, Heather knew that her thought process was different from other people, so she didn't ask people who had passed the exam for advice or compare herself to them. Destiny was purposeful to avoid people who were talking negatively about the exam. She had to recognize these negative messages and avoid them. She even shifted her own ways of thinking and talking about the exam. This concept – taking control of the relationships network of licensure exams – is counterintuitive. We typically think of test preparation and test-taking as individual, solitary activities. But they are not, or they need not be. We dive deeper into this approach in Chapter 3 and focus on how to build your test preparation network.

Conclusion and Moving Forward

This chapter began with the idea that some people are born as good standardized test-takers and others are not. This idea often means handling time-pressured situations, unfamiliar environments, and early mornings to demonstrate knowledge. To push back against this idea, this chapter gave a close analysis of three students who passed their licensure exam after initially failing. We can see from Shonda, Heather, and Destiny that success after failing wasn't a matter of doubling-down on studying, making better guesses, or avoiding the challenge. There were specific practices and changes they initiated between failing and passing. The application and extension activities that follow this chapter have you consider the ways you are similar to and different from the three students in this chapter and mindsets/behaviors to emulate or avoid. Additionally, the application and extension focuses on the four themes that cut across the students and has you evaluate yourself in each of these areas. These exercises will initiate the kind of reflection and self-evaluation that will intensify as you move through the application and extension activities deeper into this book.

Application and Extension: Reflection and Self-Evaluation

This chapter application and extension builds upon some of the ideas in Chapter 2. Specifically, we'll focus on how you see yourself in comparison to the three focal students and where you see yourself with regard to some of the key themes in the chapter.

Exercise 1

In what ways are you similar to and different from the three students in Chapter 2? Think about their experiences with standardized tests and licensure exams, their perspectives and thoughts, and how they approached the challenge. Think about specific statements they made that might resonate with you, or specific statements that you might oppose. Feel free to flip back through the chapter and scan the direct quotations from them. Think about the different ways they processed and made sense of their experiences and how these compare to your processes. How do you see yourself as similar to or different from them? Write in Table 2.2 overleaf to capture your thoughts.

Next, let's think about perspectives, practices, beliefs or thoughts from them to emulate or avoid. For example, Shonda went into the exam unprepared – twice! That's probably something to avoid. Destiny looked back on her experience and was grateful it happened. That attitude is probably healthy to emulate. As before, flip back through the chapter and skim the profiles of each student to think through what you should emulate and what you should avoid. Use Table 2.3 overleaf to capture your thoughts.

Exercise 2

Table 2.4 on p. 36 is organized by the four themes across students' experiences in Chapter 2. The grid breaks down three categories of growth (passive, active, and advanced) across these themes. Some of the bullet points in these categories come directly from Shonda, Heather, and Destiny. Others are extensions of these themes. Use the grid to evaluate

Table 2.2   Comparison Among Students

Student	Similarities to you	Differences from you
Shonda		
Heather		
Destiny		

Table 2.3   Actions to Emulate and Avoid

Student	To emulate	To avoid
Shonda		
Heather		
Destiny		

Table 2.4 Categories of Growth Across Themes

Theme	Passive	Active	Advanced
Targeted and proactive preparation	• Unsure of material on the exam. • Unsure of where you stand with respect to material on the exam. • Takes exam unprepared, possibly "just to see what it's like." • Uses no test preparation material or has too many resources, overwhelmed by them. • Believes some people are good at standardized tests and some are not.	• Aware of material covered on exam, focuses on most of it. • Knows what is on the exam from test overviews provided by test company. • Reflects upon and evaluates their preparation approaches and actions, "What's working and what isn't?"	• Focus on specific areas of weakness, not all material on exam. • Focuses on areas connected to potential points on exam; gives less attention to area with fewer potential points on exam. • Uses specific test preparation materials in strategic ways. • Makes changes to preparation approach based upon reflection and evaluation. • Puts in effort regardless of beliefs about standardized test abilities.
Unconventional strategies and test wiseness	• Relies on "test-taking strategies" instead of content knowledge. • Uses only conventional test-taking approaches (e.g., steps and procedures).	• Relies on a combination of content knowledge and test wiseness strategies. • Uses a combination of conventional and unconventional strategies (e.g., logic, estimation, insight).	• Selects and uses specific test wiseness strategies because of their desired outcome (e.g., reduce time, choose correct answer, etc.); does not apply them blindly. • Uses a combination of conventional and unconventional test-taking approaches (e.g., logic, estimation, insight) even while anxious and nervous.

Optimal test space and time	• Does not consider the impact time of day has on test experience. • Does not consider the impact of taking multiple tests in same day.	• Takes the test at a time in the day most conducive for self. • Splits up multiple tests into separate days, if helpful.	• Considers the ideal time of the semester to take exam (e.g., during a holiday break). • Takes multiple tests separately in a strategic order that benefits self.
Social circles and messages	• Open to all messages and information about self and the exam. • Or, closed to all messages and information about self and the exam.	• Seeks relevant information from other people. • Relies mostly on "strong" ties (i.e., close friends) for information and support.	• Seeks out people who can lend help with specific needs and resources. • Relies on both "strong" and "weak" relational ties for information and support. • Applies a critical filter to negative or unhelpful information; cuts off communication about exam with some people, if necessary.

where you are with each of these themes. You won't necessarily fit into one category, of course. Categories like these are thinking tools. If your perspectives or actions match some of the bullets in the "passive" or "active" columns, realize there is opportunity for growth. Consider the ideas and actions in the "advanced" column as the ones you want to develop.

Notes

1 Drew H. Gitomer, Terran L. Brown, and John Bonett, "Useful Signal or Unnecessary Obstacle? The Role of Basic Skills Tests in Teacher Preparation," *Journal of Teacher Education* 62, no. 5 (2011): 431–45.
2 Jason Millman, Carol H. Bishop, and Robert Ebel, "An Analysis of Test-Wiseness," *Educational and Psychological Measurement* 25 (1965): 707–26.
3 Millman, Bishop, and Ebel, "An Analysis of Test-Wiseness"; Irving P. McPhail, "Why Teach Test Wiseness?," *Journal of Reading* 25, no. 1 (1981): 32–8.
4 Ann M. Gallagher and Richard De Lisi, "Gender Differences in Scholastic Aptitude Test: Mathematics Problem Solving Among High-Ability Students," *Journal of Educational Psychology* 86, no. 2 (1994): 204–11; Keena Arbuthnot, "The Effects of Stereotype Threat on Standardized Mathematics Test Performance and Cognitive Processing," *Harvard Education Review* 79, no. 3 (2009): 448–72.
5 Millman, Bishop, and Ebel, "An Analysis of Test-Wiseness."
6 Mark Granovetter, "The Strength of Weak Ties: A Network Theory Revisited," *Sociological Theory* 1 (1983): 201–33.

Spiders and Their Webs   3
Advice Networks for Licensure Exams

One of my favorite science facts is that the silk spiders use to make their webs can be some of the strongest material on the plant. If you've been in the woods and accidentally walked through a spider's web, you've likely felt the strength of the silk. It doesn't snap like a thin thread when you pull on it. It bends and stretches, defying your attempts to pull it off your pant leg, sleeve, or face. This strength allows spiders to spin webs in a variety of shapes and in different terrains. Most common are orb webs. They are beautiful, symmetrical wheels with spokes equal distance from one another separated by segments. These are the most common webs. Grass spiders make webs that are different from orbs. They are a dense mess of jumbled crisscrosses in a three-dimensional funnel among blades of grass. Other spiders are minimalists. They spin a web made up of a single thread of silk and hang it between two points like a fishing line.

Each of these webs has a different function. With their size and location between bushes or branches, orb webs are designed to catch prey – especially ones that fly – while the spider waits safely out of sight on the edge of the web for an unlucky insect that might get caught. Funnel webs do not ensnare a prey in its web but rather allow a speedy spider with lethal venom to surprise an insect, bite it, and drag it back into the funnel for mealtime. The narrow end of the funnel also allows the spider an escape route in case there is a hungry frog sitting on the other side of that insect. A horizontal line web that catches a prey does not cover the area of an orb web, but it takes less time and energy to make. If a human happens to walk through and break the web, the spider can spin-up another in not too much time. The important take-away is this: spiders make different shaped webs for different purposes.

With apologies to arachnophobes, I begin this chapter talking about spiders and silk because we often ignore the web of relationships, information, and advice in which people prepare for their licensure exam. We frequently think of exam preparation as an individual process. And there is a good reason for this thinking. You register for the exam as an individual, sit to take it as an individual, and receive a score that is supposed to represent you alone. You may study with other people or get encouragement from others before taking the exam, but these are small collective steps in the midst of many individual ones – like each member of the Fellowship of the Ring carefully crossing the Bridge of Khazad Dum, alone. However, I want to challenge this individual perspective on exams and illustrate how they take place in a web of people and ideas. We saw hints of this in the previous chapter as Shonda, Heather, and Destiny prepared to retake the exam. Although they had to take the exam alone, it was through relationships with key people that they received information, ideas, support, and encouragement. Some of this information helped them to think differently about themselves; other pieces of information changed how they went about preparing for the exam or how they took it. Of course, not all information is healthy, and Destiny refrained from conversation with negative perspectives. Information and resources traveled through a network, or what we will call an "advice network." Like the different kinds of spider webs, however, not all advice networks are the same. Some are like the orb web: they are wide and expansive, reaching out in all different directions and loosely connecting people. Others are like the funnel web: they are tight-knit and dense. And yet others are simply a connection to one person, like a single thread of silk.

The purpose of this chapter is to help make advice networks more visible and understand how their different configurations can enable or deter the flow of information and resources you need. Understanding advice networks will then put you in a position of strength by helping you be more strategic about building and shaping an advice network that works for you.

Advice Networks

Just as both silk and the web it creates can have different properties, so can advice networks and the relationships in them. For decades, scholars have studied social networks and tried to understand the principles at work within them.[1] The concept of social networks here does not refer to

Facebook and other online sites, though there are many studies about these newer networks. Scholars have looked at networks of doctors and health providers, unemployed people searching for jobs, political activists, and more. How do messages and information travel most efficiently between groups of people? What kinds of networks facilitate social movements or medical innovations? Some of these principles deal with the density of the network, or how many connections there are among the people in them. Other principles deal with the strength of the relational ties, or how close to one another people are. We'll go a bit deeper into these principles below before applying them to teacher licensure exams.

In some networks, there are many connections among the people that make up that network. Everybody knows everybody, or close to it. These are high-density networks. They are like funnel webs: many of the points are connected through thick crisscrosses. Oftentimes people in these networks have strong ties among each other. People have known one another for longer periods of time, trust one another, care about each other, have reciprocity among one another.[2] A close group of friends or a sports team is usually a dense network with strong ties. These kinds of networks have some advantages. They are typically stable,[3] affording emotional support to help you persist through difficult times. If you think about a difficult time and the people who helped you get through it, they were likely part of your dense, connected network with strong ties. These kinds of networks, however, have some weaknesses. Since everyone is connected, the network can become closed off to new information. In fact, the same ideas can circulate through a dense and connected network. If these ideas are from people who share strong ties, the ideas can be hard to ignore. And over time, people in dense networks of strong ties tend to take on similar ideas, opinions, and beliefs. This principle plays out in many friend groups: over time, you grow to share many of the same opinions. When this quality increases, a friend group can fragment away from other social connections.[4]

Not all networks are dense and full of strong ties among members. Some networks are low-density, or more open. Although people exist in a network together, not all of them are directly connected with one another. There is an absence of possible ties. The network spreads out like a broad orb web rather than like a tight funnel web. Oftentimes low-density networks are made up of diverse people who have a variety of backgrounds and experiences. This diversity can be along the lines of race and ethnicity, employment position, socioeconomic class, educational experiences, political perspectives, and more. Or in a diverse network, a person might know a different baked chicken recipe than you, or a faster way to drive downtown. These kinds of networks have some disadvantages. Low-density networks are less stable than high-density networks, so they offer less support over time. Low-density networks typically have weaker ties among people – people have not known one another for long periods of time nor made significant investment in one another. Consequently, low-density networks do not offer the same kinds of support that high-density ones do. They are less likely to offer emotional support and are less equipped to help a person learn the social norms of a community or space. You may learn a new baked chicken recipe in a low-density network, but the network is not likely to help you get through a difficult time in life.

However, low-density networks and the weak ties within them have some benefits. Because there are fewer connections among members, these networks are less likely to exist as closed information loops. As noted in the previous chapter, scholars have called this principle "the strength of weak ties."[5] Even though the ties in the network are weak (meaning, people do not have a strong affinity for one another) and are less durable, they have a hidden strength: new information and ideas flowing among them. A series of studies in various fields have looked at the strength of weak ties, illustrating their role in technology innovations,[6] job acquisition,[7] negotiating crises,[8] and more. Networks also have an important impact on the experiences of new teachers and how they navigate their initial years in the classroom. Open, diverse networks tend to help teachers innovate their practice, while dense and connected networks offer new teachers support and security.[9]

Networks on the Mat

I can illustrate the impact of advice networks on our ability to develop knowledge, skills, and support by briefly sharing about a network that was important to me my final year in college: my college wrestling team. I went to a small liberal arts college outside of Chicago that had an NCAA Division III wrestling team. I had participated in the sport since junior high and won all-state honors in high-school, so I decided to join the team in college. In each of my first three years in college, I won more matches than I lost and occasionally placed at tournaments. But I never won a tournament and never came close to qualifying for the national championship tournament. I made incremental improvements each year but never made a significant jump in performance despite all of the hard work I was putting in. All of this changed my senior year.

To understand why this changed, it is important to understand a few things about the sport of wrestling beyond the spandex uniforms and cauliflower ear. Wrestling is one of the oldest sports in the world. It developed over thousands of years and centers on technique, body position, and muscle memory. As in Judo and other martial arts, little things make big differences, like the smallest angle or the slightest placement of your hips, head, or foot. While a coach is critical to any sport, the teammates who you train with every day are often the most important resources to refining your technique. Teammates and training partners are an advice network. Sometimes this advice happens by showing different technique adjustments picked up years prior. Other times it happens through correcting one another's mistakes while drilling moves together. Constant feedback and accurate information are important. This feedback can also happen when you compete against one another in practice. This is when wrestlers learn more about how their techniques work in real situations and where there might be flaws. When moves and techniques don't work as intended, it presents wrestlers with a technical problem that needs to be solved.

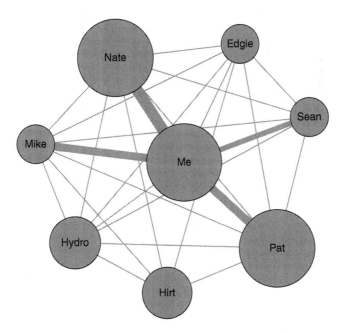

Figure 3.1   Wrestling Team Network Before Senior Year

Figure 3.1 illustrates the advice network of my team up until senior year. This is not the entire team – just the people with whom I mainly practiced. This is a dense network with connections between each person. The network took this shape because as teammates, we spent many hours together through grueling practices and traveling on road trips over the weekends to competitions. Many people on the team also lived together as roommates. Some of us even had the same majors, including education. As a result, there were facets of college life that reinforced the strong teammate ties in our network. This dense network afforded many strengths. We helped one another deal with athletic setbacks in productive ways, supported each other through relationship and personal problems, and studied together when we had the same classes.

There are other details of significance in this figure. The thickness of each line that connects us represents how frequently I practiced with certain people on the team. Thicker lines mean I practiced with someone more often and thus had a stronger tie with him. From this figure, you can see that I practiced the most with Nate, Mike, Pat, and Sean. My ties were the strongest with them. I would occasionally practice with other people on the team, but these were the four people I worked with the most and from whom I got the most consistent feedback. These people influenced me differently, however, because they were of different skill levels. Nate, Pat, and I were on about the same skill level compared to the other people on the team. So Nate and Pat influenced me more than the others. The size of each circle represents the different degrees of influence for me. Each of us on the team had been connected to yet another network in our previous high school teams, but I've left these off of the figure for sake of clarity.

A few things changed in this network at the start of my senior year of college, as you can see in Figure 3.2. Two of the people I had the strongest ties to, Pat and Mike, decided not to come back to the team. Most significantly, someone transferred into the program who was practically better than all of us combined. Dan was an undefeated high school state champion who competed on many international teams as he was growing up. On these teams, he trained with other top wrestlers from across the country and had Olympic-caliber coaches. He was awarded a scholarship to wrestle at an NCAA Division 1 program where he was surrounded by other top-level athletes. He spent two years at a Division 1 program and then decided he didn't want to continue in the sport. He was burned out. He took a year off from college and then transferred into our small college with no intention of continuing his athletic career. He ultimately decided to join our team, less for the sport and more as a way to make friends as a new student on campus. No surprise to us, Dan was an undefeated national champion while on our team.

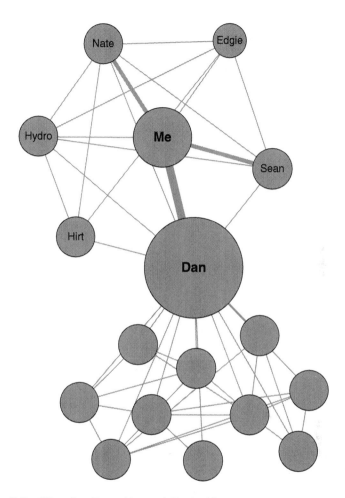

Figure 3.2 Wrestling Team Network Senior Year

Dan's presence changed the network of our team. Few of us had strong ties to Dan. We hadn't known him for very long or had time to develop reciprocal friendship and trust with him like we had with one another – the stuff of strong ties over years. During most of the year, we had weak ties with him. But the addition of his weak ties (making our network less dense) allowed for new knowledge, information, and feedback about technique to flow into the network. We all learned a great deal from him. This was especially the case for me since I practiced with him often (see the thick line between us). This knowledge and information was a product of the open and diverse network he had been in as a Division 1 athlete. He was frequently with other athletes on his level, as illustrated by the open network attached to him in Figure 3.2. The other members of our team had been connected to other networks as well, but there were lower levels of skill and knowledge in these networks.

The effects of Dan's presence in our network had the most significant effect on my performance that year (thus the size of his circle). Working with him helped me to correct small yet vital errors in technique I had been making and to learn different sets of techniques to expand my skillset. That year, I moved past the plateau I had been on, winning tournaments and qualifying to compete in the national championship tournament. In the tie between us, information flowed both ways. I didn't have much new technique to share with Dan, but he absorbed healthier ways to think about his relationship with the sport from training with me. Those ideas enabled him to recommit to the sport and not burn out.

This brief trip into college sports illustrates some of the key principles of social networks and how they operate. First, it was through a *weak tie* with Dan that I became connected to a new network of more knowledge and expertise. This knowledge and expertise helped me improve beyond what was previously attainable in my team. Second, I still benefited from those strong relational ties and the dense network of my team. Those qualities of the network helped me get through challenges that year. But, the weak tie with Dan was a small change that had a meaningful outcome. Third, it stands to reason by these social network principles that if my team network were even more open and diverse – especially earlier on – we all would have gotten much better.

Exam Advice Networks: Four Cases

Different networks are useful for different purposes. The kind of network that was useful for my purpose above was dense with strong ties among members but balanced out by some weaker ties and more open portions. Such a network provided the support that was necessary to persist through difficult times, but it also allowed for some new information about wrestling technique to flow into the network. Although the network was dense, it was not a closed loop that prevented new information from entering. Teacher licensure exams are not like college wrestling teams, so we can't assume that this kind of network is best for students studying to be teachers. This comparison, however, raises questions. What are the qualities of networks that help people prepare for teacher licensure exams? Are some networks more advantageous than others? These questions seem rather straightforward, but their answers depend upon a number of different personal qualities. The needs of one person might be very different from the needs of another, so the network qualities that will assist them are also different. One size network doesn't fit all. We can formulate some useful answers to these questions by looking at four students with different needs and the licensure exam advice networks around them. As you read these cases, think about how the different advice networks compare to your own.

Tammy: Networked in a Web of Support and Struggle

We briefly met Tammy in Chapter 1 and learned that she passed the reading and writing portions of the exam on her first attempt. However, she did not pass the math portion. She prepared diligently to retake the exam by studying with a math professor and going over materials by herself. She also explored other students' experiences with the exam by making a short survey and distributing it to people in her program. She retook the math exam twice but ultimately decided to discontinue with the major because she had not yet passed the exam. Looking at the advice network around Tammy's experience illustrates a fuller picture of her preparation.

Figure 3.3 illustrates Tammy's exam advice network. Tammy had a small advice network made up of three people, each of whom were students in the teacher education program. Each of the people knew one another, so her network was dense even though it was small – like an orb web with connected parts. She had strong ties to each of the people in her network and received information from them, as illustrated by the thickness of the arrow between them. She said she knew Kia and Yolanda "well" and Corinne "very well." Furthermore, each of the people in her network was influential on her preparation, as indicated by the size of their respective circle in the figure. Kia and Yolanda were "somewhat" influential and Corinne was "very influential." Finally, each of these people knew one another, creating a dense, connected network.

Tammy communicated with the people in her network multiple times a week about the licensure exam. They spoke in courses they had together, during study groups, and in private conversations. The most common topic of conversation was their experiences with the exam. Since Yolanda and Kia had also failed portions of the exam and were preparing for retakes, conversations about the exam included their hopes to pass, some

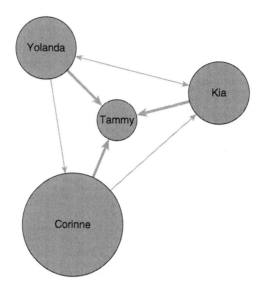

Figure 3.3 Tammy's Advice Network

frustrations about the exam, and fears about having to change their major if they did not pass the exam. Tammy also spoke with Corinne about her experience with the exam, but they also spoke about the level of difficulty of the exam and advice about how to pass.

How might the qualities of Tammy's small, dense, and connected network have shaped her preparation? As I noted above, strong ties typically help people persist through difficult times.[10] Tammy's network was made up of strong ties, and these supported her ongoing study efforts toward retaking the exam. She shared comradery particularly with Kia and Yolanda since they were all working diligently (and desperately) to pass the exam. These strong relational ties helped Tammy persist.

Yet, the density of Tammy's network also held her back in some ways. In the midst of strong relational ties, Tammy's network was a closed, dense one with little opportunity for new information to come into it. What made this closed network even more detrimental to her preparation was that other members like Yolanda and Kia had not passed the exam either. (Tammy did not say if Corinne had taken or passed the exam). In other words, Tammy's network surrounded her with struggle. She only knew of a few people who had passed the exam. Although she hoped for the best for Yolanda and Kia, she noted that working closely with them made her feel less confident about passing the exam.

Tammy's perspective on standardized exams illustrates some of the negative effects of her dense and connected network. During an interview with her, she described her frustration with preparing to retake the exam.

> I do think there's a trick. You have to know how to take a test. There's a method – I don't know it. I'm still struggling to learn the method myself. There is, there's a way to take them. And I just don't know the trick. And I never did. You know, here I am 42 years later, I've taken tests for a long time, and I still don't really get the method.

There are a few notable points in Tammy's statement. The first is that Tammy invokes her age and generational status as reasons for her struggles to pass the math portion of the licensure exam. This is an important detail that we should not miss in her statement, which I will return to in the next chapter. Second and relevant to the topic at hand, Tammy subscribes to a fixed mindset about standardized test abilities.[11] From this perspective, you either know how to take the test, or you don't. Some people learn the "tricks," and others like her – simply don't. Of course, the students' successes in the previous chapter illustrate something much different. When we look at the qualities of Tammy's preparation network, this perspective makes sense. She was surrounded by struggle and people who could not comprehend "the trick" despite their efforts. Tammy saw herself and her struggle reflected in the people around her.

Brooke: Little Support but Little Need

Brooke was in the same teacher education program as Tammy, yet the two women were not in one another's advice networks. A transfer student, Brooke took the exam during her Sophomore year. She passed on her first attempt with high scores and was on her way to pursuing her elementary education major. She put a lot of effort into studying for standardized exams in high school and into preparing for the licensure exam. She likened them to a game: "If you play by their rules, you can do well." And she did. She noted, "I have done well on my standardized test, but I work hard to do well on them."

Figure 3.4 illustrates Brooke's advice network. Her network was made up of five people: classmates in her program and teachers who she met while

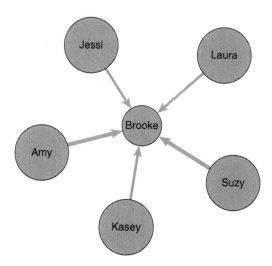

Figure 3.4   Brooke's Advice Network

completing field hours connected to some of her courses. Brooke had strong relational ties with two people her network, as indicated by the slightly thicker lines connecting her with Suzy and Amy. She felt she knew them "very well." Her ties to the others in her network were not as strong, feeling she knew them "somewhat well." Unlike in Tammy's network, however, none of the people in Brooke's network knew one another. Her network was open with very low density – less of a spider web and more of some loose threads of silk dangling out from her. Despite these different relational strengths with people in her network, Brooke felt each of them "only somewhat" influenced her preparation, thus their circles have the same size in her figure.

Brooke only spoke about the exam a few times with the people in her network. In class or in social settings, they shared personal experiences with the exam and how easy or difficult they felt it was. They told her the exam wasn't very difficult and that she would "be fine." Suzy also shared what she knew about other people's experiences, and Amy talked about some of the logistics about the exam. She noted that each of the people in her network, except for Jessi, made her feel more confident about passing the exam (Jessi, she noted, had no effect).

One of the potential drawbacks of Brooke's open network with fewer strong relational ties is that it didn't offer her much support to help her persist. However, what we know about Brooke suggests that she didn't need much support in this area. She believed that one could prepare for standardized tests. She stopped short of calling it "a trick" as Tammy did but instead thought it was a game that one *could* prepare for. She had a history of taking the initiative to prepare for standardized tests, and these efforts paid off. They continued through taking her licensure exam as she checked out some study materials from the library to get herself ready. Since she passed on her first attempt, she had no need for a dense network of strong ties to get her ready for a retake or pick her up when she needed it.

Brooke's network was also populated by people who had first-hand experience passing the exam. These people gave her enabling messages that increased her confidence in doing well. Confidence itself does not produce good performance. Sometimes people muster-up feelings of confidence in order to protect themselves from feeling unprepared in the midst of challenges. In Brooke's case, the enabling messages she received from reliable sources in her network worked in concert with her perspective on standardized exams and related preparation efforts.

Ruby: Pushed and Pulled by Strong Messages

Ruby was a classmate of Shonda, Heather, and Destiny. Like her classmates, she took the professional readiness exam for the first time during her sophomore year. She was a bit wary of the math portion of the exam because she felt it wasn't possible to prepare for an exam that covered what she perceived as a wide breadth of material. As a result, she took the reading and writing tests first and left math for later. She came close to passing reading and writing and retook them four months later and passed them both. Her reading score, in fact, went up a solid nine points. During this retake session, she also took the math test for the first time. She missed the passing score by eleven points and planned to retake the exam.

Figure 3.5 illustrates Ruby's exam preparation network. Her network was large with nine people, and she had strong ties to each person in the network by knowing them "well" or "very well." Once again, the thickness of the arrows in the figure represent the strength of relational ties. Interestingly, Ruby's network was broken into two main clusters of people: one of classmates (on the right side of the figure), and another of family members and related friends outside of college (on the left side of the figure). In fact, some of these family members had taken the exam while they were in college pursuing a teaching degree. Each of the people within these two clusters knew each other, but there were no connections across these two clusters, except for Ruby as the bridge between the two.

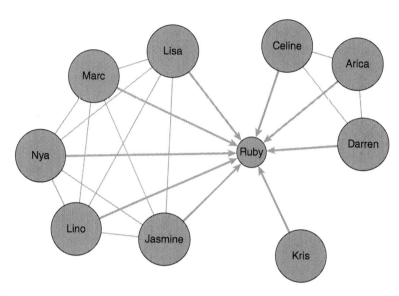

Figure 3.5 Ruby's Advice Network

Ruby reported that each person in her network was "very influential" on her preparation for the exam. What they said mattered to her, even if they only spoke a few times. Each person also made her much more confident about passing the exam – except for her brother (more on him in a minute). She communicated with these people about the exam a few times each semester through private conversations and even online through Facebook. Even though she communicated with people only a few times during the semester, this communication was full of different types of information. They touched on advice about how to prepare, personal experiences with the exam, the difficulty of the exam, strategies Ruby might use to pass, and what they heard about other people's experiences with the exam. Ruby's network was full of information about the exam, on all different angles, from people whose viewpoint mattered to her.

The qualities of Ruby's network – large and full of strong relational ties – influenced her preparation in a few ways. Because Ruby had such strong relational ties to people in her network, their experiences and perspectives mattered a great deal to her and were hard to ignore. Her sister's experience with the exam and how her brother responded to it were particularly influential to her. Two years prior, her sister Jasmine took the exam while she was pursuing a teaching degree. Their brother paid the $160 for her to take the exam. Jasmine failed the exam and decided to change her major to social work. Feeling like he wasted money, their brother responded, "I just spend $160 dollars for you!" When he learned that Ruby had to take the same exam, the experience two years ago influenced his response. Ruby recalled the exchange:

> *I'm not paying.* Like immediately when I told him, *I'm about to take the Praxis,* he's like, *Well, don't ask me for the money because your sister failed.* And I was just like, *sheesh!*

Ruby had no intention of asking her brother to pay for the exam because her college was covering the cost. However, his aggressive response was still influential to her. As I noted above, Ruby said that all of the people in her network made her much more confident about passing the exam, except for her brother. She stopped short of saying he made her less confident but instead took a neutral position on his influence. Ruby's sister encouraged her to take the exam again if she failed, but Ruby's network lacked examples of people who had done just that.

Ruby's network put her in the position of being pushed and pulled by strong messages from many people with whom she was close. Another instance of Ruby being moved by messages took place with a professor in the program who was encouraging students about the exam. Although Ruby did not place the professor in her network, the interaction was still notable. Dr. Delano offered the class a word of encouragement one Friday because they were taking the exam on Saturday: "I'm proud of you guys that's going out on Saturday to take the text. And I'm gonna ask everybody how they did." Ruby thought:

> Now, what if I fail? Like what I'm gonna tell her? You know, I'm doing so good in her class and I can't pass Praxis? You understand? So it's just like, I don't want nobody to ask me, *Yeah, what was your score?* I want to tell people, *Yeah I passed,* instead of them asking me, *Hey, how did you do? You got your score back?*

Ruby did not intend to give up on the exam after only one attempt, as her sister did. Her plan was to take the exam up to three times, and if she hadn't passed by then – change her major. This susceptibility to messages also came from the score on the exam. Ruby knew that she could retake the exam if she needed, but she wasn't clear if that first score would still count in some way after a retake. After she found out that only her highest score would count, she still felt the first score would influence her thinking and experience. "To me, it's just final," she explained, referencing the first score. "I think I'll just keep it mentally in mind."

Destiny: Network Diversity and Critical Filters

We learned about Destiny in the previous chapter: her meticulous preparation for retakes, and her ultimate success on the exams despite some challenges. A look into Destiny's exam advice network helps illustrate more about her unique trajectory to passing the exam after failing it multiple times. Destiny's network is also an important contrast to those of Tammy, Brooke, and Ruby.

Figure 3.6 represents Destiny's exam advice network. Like Ruby, her network was large with eight people. These people included classmates, a close friend, her mother, and a professor (me). As in Ruby's network, there was a cluster of students in Destiny's network, but there were fewer relational ties among these people. To recall, all of Ruby's classmates knew each other and shared information. This was not the case with Destiny's classmates. Manny wasn't connected to anyone else, and Mae was only connected to me. We can say the cluster of Destiny's classmates had a lower density compared to Ruby's. Another notable characteristic of Destiny's network is that she has two people (her mother and Manny) with no other ties to members in the network outside of their ties with Destiny. If we think about Destiny's network as a spider web, it was an unbalanced one – not densely connected like a funnel web and not equally spread out like an orb. It has some of these qualities, but also some single lines of silk, as in Brooke's network.

As illustrated by the thickness of lines from Destiny to the people in her network, she had a range of different relational strengths with them. The strongest relational ties were to Rose and me, two people who Destiny felt she knew very well, especially in context with academic pursuits and the exam. Naturally, she also recorded having a strong tie with her mother. But notably, Destiny felt the rest of the people in her network were only people she knew from class. She knew them "somewhat well" through weaker relational ties. There was also a range of influences that the people in her network had on her preparation. Unlike Ruby who was strongly influenced by every person in her network (even if she only

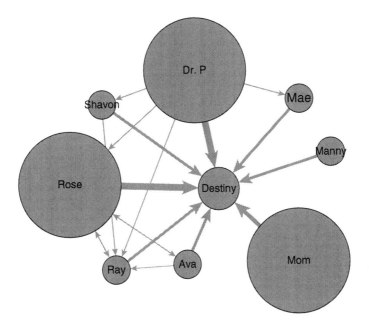

Figure 3.6 Destiny's Advice Network

communicated with them a few times during the semester), only three people in Destiny's network had a strong influence on her preparation: Rose, her mother, and me. She noted the rest of the people, though present in her network, had *no* influence on her preparation. The small circles for these people on Destiny's network represent their lack of influence.

Destiny communicated with most people in her network during social gatherings. For the people she was closest to, it was during private conversations and study sessions. However, Destiny did not receive the same kind of information from everyone. Unlike the other women, who received mostly the same kind of information from everyone in their network, Destiny received certain types of information from certain people. For example, Ava only spoke about rumors and what she had heard about the exam. Mae only gave advice and information about the exam's level of difficulty. Rose provided all different kinds of information. Table 3.1 illustrates which types of information Destiny received from whom in her network.

Table 3.1   Destiny's Information Sources

Source	General Advice	Personal experiences	Logistics	Level of difficulty/ ease	Test-taking strategies	Rumors	Info about others' experiences
Mae	X			X			
Shavon	X			X	X		
Dr. P.	X		X	X	X		
Ray							X
Ava						X	
Mom					X		
Manny	X						
Rose	X	X	X	X	X		X

Source: Author.

Why is there so much variation in terms of information in Destiny's network? Destiny was able to get certain kinds of information from some people by applying a critical filter to the messages around her. She didn't simply take what information came her way. We touched on this in the previous chapter when Destiny spoke about identifying negative messages around her and avoiding those conversations. She spoke further about this approach by comparing it to how her close friend Rose treated information about the exam.

> Rose for instance, she listens to what other people say like, if someone said they took the test, she'd be like, *Was it easy, was it hard?* And I'm like, *You're different from them. I don't think you should listen to what –* Like, I don't listen to what other people say when they say that the computer version is harder, or this thing is harder – because I know I'm different. So I'm not going to necessarily think that's going to be harder.

Unlike Ruby, this critical filter protected Destiny from being too heavily influenced by the opinions of people around her. She was able to have people in her network but reduce their influence upon her if their messages did not support her growth or fit her needs, especially if these messages came from people who she saw not preparing for the exam. The legitimacy of these people's messages was diminished in her view and easier to ignore.

As a whole, Destiny's preparation existed in a diverse network with a mixture of strong and weak ties. There were parts of her network that were dense with many connections between people, and parts that were open with fewer connections among people. The strong ties enabled her to persist when she was frustrated, stressed, or sad about retaking the exam – even for a third time. Yet, her information was not limited to a dense concentration of close ties. She had new information and advice coming from weak relational ties in her network as well, and she sought out this information through a critical filter based upon her needs.

What If? Posing Questions to the Four Cases

As I noted at the start of this chapter, each kind of network has some strengths and weaknesses. The usefulness of a network should be judged on the needs of the individual. Pulling back from these four cases, we can apply some of the principles from social networks to pose some questions and think about what might have been.

Tammy's small, high-density network poses a few questions. How might her experience have changed if her network had been more open and diverse? For instance, what if someone like Destiny or Brooke had been in Tammy's network? Destiny was like Tammy in some regards: struggling with the exam and desperately working to pass. Yet, Destiny's performance on the exam improved incrementally, and she ultimately passed. Her presence in Tammy's network would have served as a vicarious model of success: someone like Tammy – also struggling to pass the exam – but who ultimately did. These kinds of models can significantly shape the beliefs we hold about our capabilities.[12] Though vicarious models, we think, "If they can do it, maybe I can too." A weak tie with Destiny would have also given Tammy access to the wide array of ideas that helped Destiny change her practice – ideas that were not present in her close network of strong ties.

What about Brooke? Brooke's strong record of performance with standardized tests would not have made her a strong vicarious model of success for Tammy. From a distance, Brooke would have seemed like of those people who found out "the trick" to passing those exams. A relational tie with Brooke, however, could have given Tammy a different way of conceptualizing the exams and seeing beyond tricks. To recall, Brooke thought of the exam as a game with rules. If you play by those rules, you can do well. The metaphors we use to understand the world around us have a powerful influence on our behaviors and actions.[13] They afford us different ways of thinking about challenges and situations. Games can be won if we learn the rules, prepare in accordance with them, and perform well when it matters. Tricks? Magicians perform tricks through deception and secrecy. Brooke's presence in Tammy's network could have introduced a healthier way to think about the challenge of the exam.

Ruby's large network of strong ties also poses some questions. To recall, she was highly influenced by all of the people in her network – family members and friends alike. What they said mattered, and their messages were difficult to ignore. How might her experience have been different if she had developed Destiny's critical filter? Would she have been able to resist or ignore some of the messages in her network? Perhaps this filter would have lessened the extra pressure put on by her brother and her sister's experience with the exam. A critical filter would have put Ruby in control of the messages, like an orchestra conductor controlling the volume and intensity of different instruments before her.

In discussing these "what ifs," I want to be careful not to set up Destiny and Brooke as the ideal models to emulate. Their networks were appropriate *for their needs*. But if their needs had changed, the networks could have been absent of important resources. For example, Brooke needed little support from the people around her because she was a self-starter, had a history of doing well on standardized exams, and passed on her first try. She didn't receive the bad news of a low score; she wasn't forced to take the long road back to retaking the exam. If she had, however, her open network with no ties between members would have provided less support during this difficult time. She lacked the network of strong ties rallying around her to keep going. Tammy had this support. Brooke did not. Fortunately for Brooke, she didn't need it.

Reflecting on the Cases: Your Needs, Your Network

There are two different angles through which we can reflect on the four cases above. The first of these deals with which of the networks is most similar to yours. Is your network like Brooke's, wherein you have a few contacts who occasionally give ideas and information about the exam? Or is your network like Ruby's, a dense collection of people whose opinions matter a great deal to you? The second angle of reflection deals with whose predicament is most similar to yours. Perhaps you are like Tammy and feel the pressure building up all around you. Or, you might see yourself reflected in Destiny, needing to pass the exam but taking control of the network and information around you. Thinking about these networks and students as models, you might get the sense that your network needs to change from how it looks currently. The application and extension exercises that follow this chapter will help answer these questions and help you make any necessary changes to your network.

Application and Extension: Understanding Your Advice Network

The procedures below will map out your current exam advice network to identify the people from whom you get advice and information about the exam. These steps will reveal whether your network is an orb web, a funnel web, or something else. The second activity focuses on adding important details to the network, such as what kinds of information you receive from the people in your network and how close you are to them. The final procedure leads you through the analysis of your network with specific recommended steps for how to take control and make changes to it. Completing these procedures will help you to remake your exam network into something that works for you.

Exercise: Mapping Your Network

Step 1: Who Shares with Whom?

In Figure 3.7, write the names of the people who have shared information or advice with you about the licensure exam. Then, draw directional

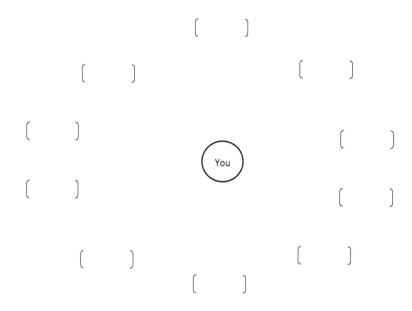

Figure 3.7 Your Advice Network

arrows among the people in the network to illustrate who shares information with whom. Draw more brackets if your network is larger than ten
people. The result should look like a type of web that illustrates who
communicates with whom.

Step 2: Informing Your Advice Network

We are going to designate a shape to each person based upon their
personal experience with the licensure exam. Draw one of the following
shapes around each person's name in your network. If you don't know
this information about the person, then you should try to find it out.

- Square: anyone who passed on their first try.
- Triangle: anyone who failed on their first try but then later passed.
- Diamond: anyone who has taken the exam but not yet passed.
- Circle: anyone who has not taken the exam or you are unsure.

Next, think about what kind of advice or information each person gives you about the exam. This information may be about personal experiences, exam difficulty/ease, strategies, logistics, or other things. Write this information next to each person's shape in Figure 3.7. Below is an example of what these steps might look like. Note the square around Maya denotes that she passed the exam on her first try.

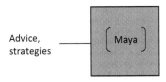

Step 3: How Influential Is Each Person?

Finally, think about how influential each person is on your feelings about the licensure exam. Some people's perspectives you hold in high regard. Others are easy to dismiss. Rate each person on the following scale, and write the corresponding number underneath their name in their shape:

1	2	3	4	5
(not at all)	(not very)	(somewhat)	(influential)	(very influential)

Step 4: Analyzing Your Network

Following the previous steps, you've mapped your licensure exam network, identified people's experiences with the exam, and identified how influential everyone's opinion and perspective is to you. There's more. It is not enough simply to see and understand the network. The real growth comes when you can analyze your network and then shape and alter it based upon your needs. We saw Destiny take these steps in the previous chapter. Use Table 3.2 to do the same.

Table 3.2 Changes to Advice Network

Analyze . . .	If . . .	Then . . .	Notes
The shape and density of your network. Is your network an orb, a funnel web, or a few single threads? Are there dense clusters, disconnected members, or both? How many people are in your network?	Your network is very dense (i.e., everyone is connected to everyone).	• Get to know new people and their experiences with the exam. • Ask people outside of your friend group and network if you can interview them about their experiences. Use some ideas in the application and extension from Chapter 5 to develop interview questions. Consider both face-to-face and online.	• These new network members should be weak ties (i.e., not close friends). • Be careful about believing everyone. Apply a critical filter to the new information you learn. • Be sure these new people do not have many connections to your current network, otherwise they will only add more density to your already-dense network.
	Your network is very open (i.e., everyone is disconnected).	• Connect some of the people in your network. Ask them to meet for a meal or over coffee to share advice and experiences about the exam. Get them talking to one another. • Form a study and advice group that meets weekly. Specify the purpose and norms of the meetings beforehand so they do not become spaces for complaining or talking only about negative experiences.	• Seek a variety of experiences with the exam for a study and advice group. Be sure there are a variety of "shapes" from Step 2 in the group.

The main kinds of information you receive from the people in your network. What kind of information do you get the most? What kind of information do you get the least? What kind of information do you need more of?	You are missing some specific types of information in your network.	• Ask people already in your network for that kind of information. • Seek this information from new people outside of your network that you do not know well (i.e., weak ties). • Develop a list of five questions that you can ask people to get you the kind of information you need. • Over time, people in dense networks tend to share the same information. The new information might be in your network, but you just have to ask for it and go beyond the familiar way of interacting with one another. • Apply a critical filter to the new information you get. Ask yourself, does this seem like it would work for me?
The range of experience people in your network have with the exam (i.e., the shapes you drew around people's names). What shapes appear most and least in your network? Which are missing? Are you surrounded by people who struggle with the exam? Do you have people in your network who have passed? Do you have people who have overcome struggles?	Your network is mostly people of one particular experience with the exam (e.g., passed on first try, haven't passed at all, etc.).	• Seek out people with different experiences with the exam that you can learn from. • Do this by asking about people's experiences, both face-to-face and online, and requesting a short interview with them. • Build a network of people whose experience with the exam is both similar to and different from your own. • Networking through the many education hashtag chats on Twitter can be a great way to work outside of your existing network. • Be specific about what you're asking for. For example, you might ask if anyone passed their licensure exam after initially failing and if they would be willing to talk with you about their experience. People typically enjoy talking about their experiences. You can follow up by email or direct messages.

(Continued)

Table 3.2 (Cont.)

Analyze . . .	If . . .	Then . . .	Notes
How influential people are on your feelings about the exam. Look at the numbers you have assigned to each person. Is it all 5s in your network? All 1s? Or is there a mixture?	You have mostly 5s in your network.	• Consider how each of these people influence you and if the presence of many strong influences may pull you in too many directions. • Set boundaries around with whom you will talk about the licensure exam, especially if certain people reduce your confidence, increase your anxiety, or influence you to think negatively/complain.	• Setting boundaries does not mean you cannot still be friends with some people. You simply exclude them from your exam network by privately deciding not to interact with them about the topic.

You have mostly 1s in your network.

- Consider how you may need people in your network who have a strong and positive influence on you and can support you in challenging times.
- Consider the reasons why some people do not have a strong influence on you and if there is helpful advice that should have a stronger influence on you.

- Sometimes there are good reasons for a person to be uninfluential (e.g., they give bad advice or lack expertise). Other times, their advice is good but you are uninfluenced by it because you believe they are very different from you (e.g., "good" test-taker vs. "bad" test-taker). It's important to dig beneath these surface assumptions and learn how you are similar to other people who can be a strong, positive influence.

Notes

1 Kira Baker-Doyle, "No Teacher Is an Island: How Social Networks Shape Teacher Quality," in *Promoting and Sustaining a Quality Teacher Workforce* (Bingley, UK: Emerald Group, 2015), 367–83; Alan J. Daly, ed., *Surveying the Terrain Ahead: Social Network Theroy and Educational Change* (Cambridge, MA: Harvard Education Press, 2010).

2 Mark Granovetter, "The Strength of Weak Ties: A Network Theory Revisited," *Sociological Theory* 1 (1983): 201–33.

3 Nan Lin, "Social Networks and Status Attainment," *Annual Review of Sociology* 25 (1999): 467–87; Ronald S. Burt, "Structural Holes versus Network Closure as Social Capital," in *Social Capital: Theory and Research* (New Brunswick, NJ: Transaction Publishers, 2001), 31–56.

4 Mark Granovetter, "The Strength of Weak Ties: A Network Theory Revisited," *Sociological Theory* 1 (1983): 201–33.

5 Ibid.

6 Morten T. Hansen, "The Search-Transfer Problem: The Role of Weak Ties in Sharing Knowledge Across Organization Subunits," *Administrative Science Quarterly* 44, no. 1 (1999): 82–111.

7 Mark Granovetter, *Getting a Job: A Study of Contact and Careers* (Cambridge, MA: Harvard University Press, 1974).

8 David Krackhardt and Robert N. Stern, "Informal Networks and Organizational Crises: An Experimental Simulation," *Social Psychology Quarterly* 51, no. 2 (1988): 123–40.

9 Kira Baker-Doyle, *The Networked Teacher: How New Teachers Build Social Networks for Professional Support* (New York, NY: Teachers College Press, 2011).

10 Nan Lin, "Social Networks and Status Attainment."

11 Carol S. Dweck, *Mindset: The New Psychology of Success* (New York, NY: Penguin Random House, 2006).

12 Albert Bandura, *Self-Efficacy: The Exercise of Self Control* (New York, NY: Worth Publishers, 1997).

13 George Lakov and Mark Johnson, *Metaphors We Live By* (Chicago, IL: University of Chicago Press, 1980).

Part 2

Addressing What's Felt but Not Seen

Say You're White and You'll Definitely Pass

4

Working Through Ideas About Cultural Bias and Tests

Ashley sat down at a regional testing center to take her professional readiness exam for the fifth time. She needed to score two points higher on the math portion of the exam for admittance into the capstone teaching internship during her final semester of senior year. Although she had not yet passed each portion of the exam, she had been working diligently, taking advantage of tutoring opportunities, and making progress each semester. As an African American woman, Ashley drew motivation from history, her ancestors, and her race. She knew that many of her ancestors were denied the educational opportunities now afforded to her. "That's my motivation to succeed," she said, and it showed through in her efforts to pass the exam. Because of this effort and progress, the professors at her institution had given her provisional entrance into the program with the expectation and hope that she would pass all portions of the exam before it was time for the senior year internship. That time had come; she needed to pass, and she was almost there.

In the computerized version of the tests Ashley was taking, a demographic survey comes before the exam. With some variation, surveys like these often ask about a test-taker's age, education background, college grade point average, gender identification, and other variables. The surveys also ask about the test-taker's race and ethnicity. When Ashley was presented with this question about her race – moments before she would start the exam – she recalled a piece of information the head librarian had told her the previous semester. He talked about his wife's experience (also an African American woman) taking the same exam and the demographic survey that stared back at Ashley from the computer screen. Ashley paraphrased the librarian's advice like this:

> He said his wife took the test many times and she never passed. And then the last time she took it, she marked that she was a white woman, and she passed the last time. And that's it.

The conversation with the librarian, Mr. Holmes, came as Ashley and two of her friends were completing volunteer hours in the library as part of their Kappa Delta Pi education honors society membership. She shared the conversation with her mother as well. "The way he was telling it," Ashley explained, "It was like *Yeah, check this box and you're definitely going to pass* and things like that. *Race is definitely a factor with that test. It's biased.*"

Remembering what Mr. Holmes said about his wife, Ashley stared at the demographic survey on the screen and began contemplating which race box she should check. "I could say I was on that screen for like two or three minutes," Ashley described. "I was just going back and forth like, should I do this or should I not? Like, I don't know." As Ashley stared at the screen contemplating which race box to check, she didn't think through the technical details of how identifying as white could shape her score, such as if she would receive a different set of questions or a different scoring rubric as a "white" test-taker. She just knew that she was desperate to pass. "There was just so much stuff going through my mind, so I finally checked it just to make sure. Just to see if it could help."

Ashley went on with the exam after checking the white box, taking the allotted 75 minutes to complete the exam. When she finished, she sat and waited while the computer calculated her score. When the score came up, she exclaimed to herself, "Wow, I really just did that!" She had exceeded the passing score by two points and passed the exam.

Mr. Holmes told Ashley that "race was definitely a factor" with the exam and that she would pass the exam if she checked the white demographic box. Was he right? Is race a factor? Or, a bit more broadly, do aspects of our identities – like race, socioeconomic class, and gender – factor into licensure exam performance? Are exams biased against certain aspects of our identities? This chapter jumps into questions like these about cultural bias and unfairness in teacher licensure exams – ideas introduced by these interactions between Ashley and Mr. Holmes. The chapter unpacks some of the ways students latch onto ideas about cultural bias and how these ideas can shape the ways students experience their licensure exams. I will use two frameworks in this chapter – "Big Assumptions" and "ghosts in the room" – to help us think strategically about these experiences. Understanding where these ideas come from and how people latch onto them is crucial for moving past them.

A Closer Look at Cultural Bias

Ashley had heard from Mr. Holmes that the exam was biased, that "race was a factor." Cultural or racial bias on standardized tests is a topic that has received much attention from educators and education researchers over many years. Some of this attention comes from the scientists who create standardized tests and their highly technical studies called Differential Item Functioning, or DIF. Some of this attention also comes from scholars who focus on how standardized tests have functioned for decades to limit the employment and education opportunities for people of color and folks living in poverty.[1] As we saw with Ashley, these ideas about bias are not limited to research reports or scholarly articles. They get passed around through conversations and echo through the thoughts of some test-takers. To have a healthy understanding of this topic and standardized tests, we have to take a closer look at the meanings and misconceptions around the idea of bias. We may still reject the use of such exams after this closer look, but nonetheless it will give us a more useful way to think about bias and exams than the one that Mr. Holmes offered.

In his book *Measuring Up: What Educational Testing Really Tells Us*, Daniel Koretz offers a helpful breakdown of bias on standardized tests.[2] Koretz unpacks common misconceptions about test bias. The first of these misconceptions is that bias is an attribute of a specific test. We saw Mr. Holmes represent this misconception when he told Ashley that the test his spouse and Ashley took was biased. Koretz notes that bias is an attribute of a specific *inference* that one makes from a test, but not of the test itself. This phrasing may seem like a meaningless distinction or a slight-of-hand, so an example is in order.

My first full-time teaching position was at a high school in California only a few miles from the U.S.-Mexico border. The subject I taught was English. This means my students mostly read texts, analyzed them, and wrote about them and other topics meaningful to them. Many of my students were Mexican American and fluent in multiple languages. Although I did not teach classes intended for students who were still developing English proficiency (these were taught by educators with TESOL certifications), it was not uncommon for a few students in my "regular" English course to be only borderline proficient in the English language. Their level of proficiency came out most clearly through writing. Early on, many of the literary analysis and text-response assignments I would design were very traditional; they were written essays. That is, writing was the means for students to demonstrate their abilities to analyze and respond to texts. What's the problem here?

The problem is that my assessment conflated two skills that are actually separate: writing and literary analysis. In the assessment, students needed to be proficient in writing to demonstrate their literary analysis skills; they needed one skill to express the other. Consequently, my assessment was invalid *for making inferences about students' literary analysis skills.* More specifically, it was invalid for making inferences about students who lacked writing proficiency. Their lack of writing proficiency would mask their literary analysis abilities. Remember, in this instance I was interested in literary analysis – not writing. For students who were proficient in writing, the assessment was valid: it would allow me to make accurate inferences about their literary analysis skills. One way to remove bias from the assessment would be having students demonstrate their literary analysis verbally instead of in writing. Verbal fluency typically develops before written fluency, so this modification would correctly separate literary analysis from writing abilities. And this is what I did once I realized the assessment – for the purpose I had intended – was biased against students with developing writing proficiency. An even better modification would be to allow students to demonstrate literary analysis in whatever language they felt most fluent.

As Koretz noted, bias is about the specific inference one wants to make from a test. If I had intended the original assessment to give me information about students' writing skills, then it is not biased. The assessment would have likely given me valid information about which of my students lacked writing proficiency. I could accurately make such an inference from the results of the assessment. With this information, I could then give students more attention and support. Bias deals with the inference one makes from a test, not the test itself.

Returning to Mr. Holmes's comment, there is an important piece of information missing from his claim that "Race is definitely a factor with that text. It's biased." The missing information is *biased with respect to what inference?* We don't know the answer to this question because Mr. Holmes did not specify.

What Mr. Holmes was likely referring to – the root of his judgment – was the second misconception about bias and standardized tests: that score differences between groups automatically mean there is bias.[3] This point in itself is incorrect. Score differences between groups *might* be an indicator of bias, but differences alone do not prove bias. In the example from my English class above, score differences would indeed be produced by bias. But sometimes score differences indicate *actual* differences in knowledge and skills – not that a test is invalid for making a particular inference. Think back for a moment to my classroom in southern California near an international border. My first year of teaching there was 2001. One morning during the second week of school, word traveled through the halls that a plane had flown into one of the World Trade Center towers in New York City. "What a horrible accident!" most of us at the school thought, not yet having seen the footage. An hour later as I was on my planning period, I saw on the news channel in the staff area that a second plane had done the exact same thing to the other tower. By lunch, we knew it wasn't an accident but a terrorist attack. One of the consequences of this attack over the entire year was that the international border between the U.S. and Mexico was much tighter. Students with family a few miles away in Tijuana were unable to see them regularly, or if they did travel south over the weekend, they often had trouble getting back into the country for school on Monday, even if they were U.S. citizens.

This situation meant that students who visited family over the weekends or split time between the two countries regularly missed school on Mondays, especially the first half of the day. In my English class, that meant they missed the introduction to the week's vocabulary, something we always did on Mondays in my class in preparation for Friday's vocabulary quiz. This meant that these students – Mexican American students – starting doing poorly on vocabulary quizzes. There was distinct score gap between white and Mexican American students on vocabulary quizzes. Did this score gap mean that the vocabulary quiz was biased for measuring Mexican American students' vocabulary knowledge? In this instance, no. The quiz was measuring a real difference in vocabulary knowledge. This real difference was due to a complex interplay of my shortsighted (and unfair) classroom routines, tightening of the international border, and student mobility. I would argue that none of this was fair to students, but the score differences on the vocabulary quiz were not an indicator of bias in the test. Those differences were real.

Alternatively, Koretz also unpacks that tests can be biased even when there are no distinct score differences between groups. Many of my students were some of the hardest working students I have ever worked with. Some were first generation immigrants, undocumented immigrants, and soon-to-be first generation high school graduates and college students.

These positions and experiences often pushed them to develop an incredible work ethic in the face of some challenges, like developing proficiency in a second language. Mariana was one of these students. Barely proficient in English, she often outworked other students in class who had easier paths before them. She often came in for extra help, took every opportunity to revise essays, never missed a single assignment, and always advocated for herself. She squeaked out a 3.0 in 12th grade English to graduate with honors. In truth, her literary analysis skills were likely more developed than other students who earned the same grade in my class. But the ways that some assignments were constructed, like my poorly-conceived literary analysis assignments, likely *depressed* her scores to be *equal* with other students of *lower* skills. Her scores were misleadingly low. An assessment that was valid for indicating her skills would have shown them as superior to other students. Tests can be biased even if there are no score differences between groups.

The most useful term that would lend further clarity to Mr. Holmes's critique is *adverse impact*. Adverse impact refers to the negative effects that score differences have on the opportunities afforded to a group of people.[4] The group could be a certain race or ethnicity, a particular socioeconomic class, third graders, students in a specific school, or any other classification. The adverse impact of a test is separate from test bias. A test can be biased for a particular function and not have an adverse impact. Despite the bias of my literary analysis essay, it did not have an adverse impact on the opportunities afforded to Mariana. She still graduated (with honors) and was admitted to college. The placement of my Friday vocabulary quizzes did have an adverse impact on students traveling across the border, even though the quiz itself was not biased.

The licensure exam Ashley and Mr. Holmes's wife took may or may not be biased for a certain purpose. But because it is a gatekeeping exam, we know it has the potential to have an adverse impact – regardless of bias. When Mr. Holmes called the test biased and noted that race was a factor, he was likely referring to the negative impact the test can have on admission into teacher education programs. In his case, he was referring to African American students. He could have also made this point with regard to other students of color, or perhaps students from lower economic households.

This more precise language should not remove our concerns about if and how some exams can be biased for certain purposes. This language and the related concepts should help us to understand what we mean by bias, that bias can exist even when score differences are not present, or that score differences themselves among groups do not necessarily mean a test is biased. There are a range of positions more useful than the single one Mr. Holmes offered. We might think about how Ashley's experience could have been different if she were aware of these different positions on bias and related concepts. Perhaps these ideas would have given her room to think differently about Mr. Holmes's advice and which box to check on the demographic survey before the exam.

How Ideas of Bias Shape People's Experiences

It should be no surprise that during the 75 minutes of taking the exam, these distinctions between test bias and adverse impact were not on Ashley's mind. She was focused on the test and task before her. It wasn't until after the exam when she was relaying the experience to her mother that she began thinking about the possible impact that checking the white box might have had on her exam outcome.

"I was telling my mom about the passing thing," Ashley explained. "Like how I felt with some of the questions, how some questions I felt that I knew, how some I felt I didn't. And then it just came up . . . So I told her, *I did check it off.*"

"Oh really?" her mother replied. "Oh well."

It wasn't until the conversation with her mother that Ashley began thinking about how identifying as white on the survey might have shaped her score. "Hmm, maybe it did give me –" Ashley said, recounting her thought process at the time and how she was making sense of the box and the score. "At that point," she continued, "that's when I really started thinking."

The process at work in Ashley's sense-making here is called attribution. Attribution is an important process by which people make sense of their experiences and the causes of outcomes in the world around them. It deals with the causal explanations that people give to themselves (and others) for their successes, failures, and other outcomes. People can attribute outcomes to a variety of causes including their own efforts and hard work, the ease of a task, extra support they received, chance or luck, and more.[5] Some of these causes, like hard work and effort, are within a person's locus of control. Others, like the ease of a task or luck, are not. After the conversation with her mother, Ashley started entertaining the idea that at least part of her success – what she attributed her success to – came from something outside of her control: identifying as white in the demographic survey.

Processes of attribution are important because they influence people's subsequent actions, how they interpret challenges, and how much effort they exert in the face of challenges.[6] If I attribute making five free throws in a row to luck, then I am less likely to put in effort and practice to improve the mechanics of my shot. I'll simply shoot my free throws and hope I get lucky. Given how attribution can shape our intentions, Ashley's move to attribute her success on the exam to checking the white demographic box (rather than factors under her control, like hard work and effort) were not insignificant. This attributional move can have negative effects on a person's future effort, the preparation plans they make, and more.

Ashley shared her story of passing not only with her mother but also with two close friends in the program. Antoinette and Chanelle (also Black women) were well acquainted with Ashley's struggle to pass the exam and her efforts leading up to it. Recalling the ideas from the previous chapter, we can say that Ashley has strong relational ties with Antoinette and Chanelle. As teacher education students, they too had taken the exam, with Antoinette failing and Chanelle passing. While relaying the story of passing to her friends, Ashley revealed that she had checked the white demographic box. The two friends had very different responses. Antoinette noted that she had considered doing the same thing on her own test. Chanelle's response was much stronger, even incredulous: "I can't believe you did that! Really? Did you really do that!?"

Chanelle disapproved of Ashley's actions for two reasons. First, she knew how much effort Ashley had put toward passing the exam. She knew about the extra hours studying, the social events she had skipped, and the hours of sleep she had foregone. For Chanelle, it was an affront for Ashley to attribute success to anything but her own effort and sacrifice. To reach for something as frivolous as a demographic box made it worse. Second, Chanelle took exception to Ashley, a Black woman, temporarily suspending her own race to identify as white on the survey – especially since Ashley took inspiration from her African American identity and ancestors.

Chanelle made her position clear to Ashley in the midst of an emotional exchange during class a few weeks after the exam. Surrounded by a small group of peers and their professor (me), she called out Ashley for checking the white box and made her come clean to the rest of the class. Her purpose in doing this, however, was not malice. It was to shift Ashley's process of attribution and re-center it on what actually enabled her to pass: her own hard work and dedication. During this emotional exchange, Chanelle recounted to Ashley all of the sacrifices she had made leading up to the exam. The rest of the class (myself included) followed suit, pointing out to Ashley the hard work and effort that went into her passing the exam.

This intense conversation pushed Ashley to shift her process of attribution. It helped her believe that her success on the exam was a result of her efforts and nothing else. The conversation with classmates and this new attributional process changed how Ashley went about preparing for the writing portion of the exam that she took a few weeks after the math portion. She described this new attribution process and its effects:

> So at that point, I just took everything Chanelle told me, like the truth, and I just pushed it and worked hard. Then when it came to that question when I took the writing test, I just did the right answer. I wasn't even thinking. It was like without hesitation, I just put "African American."

> After Chanelle said all the work I was doing to prepare for the test, I did the same amount of work to prepare for the writing test the last time I took it. So I guess for the first time, I was desperate. I would do anything. And the last time, I knew that I had it. Like I had another level of confidence.

Instead of attributing her success to something external like the demographic box, Ashley saw that it was her diligent study habits and sacrifices that made her successful. Attributing her success to these practices gave her "another level of confidence" when taking the writing exam. Of course, confidence is tricky. At times, people attempt to muster-up feelings of confidence as a method of coping with stress or to avoid feeling unprepared. Sometimes people still fail even when they are confident. Many times people pass when they do not feel confident. The important take-away for Ashley was that she understood it wasn't luck, checking a certain demographic box, or something else that helped her to pass. She passed because of the effort she put in.

What lessons can we take away from Ashley's experiences? Ashley's journey from Mr. Holmes's comment about test bias to reassessing the root of her success illustrates how influential ideas about test bias can be upon people as they take exams. Even comments made in passing can have an influence on test-takers' actions in the moment and how they make sense of their experiences after the exam. Fortunately for Ashley, she had people in her exam advice network (see the previous chapter) who could help shift her process of attribution into one that was more healthy. Ashley's story also underscores how important it is to have a critical filter for the information and advice that exists in one's network – a point we learned from Destiny in the previous chapter.

Ideas about Self: Big Assumptions and Ghosts in the Room

It is not only ideas about test bias that can shape how students experience taking their exam. Ideas about specific groups of test-takers, including ones they belong to, can also be powerful influences upon students and how they experience the testing process. Sometimes these ideas are the result of years of experience with various standardized tests dating back to elementary school. We saw some indications of this phenomenon earlier in this book while learning about Tammy's struggles to pass the exam. Tammy's status as an older student shaped how she made sense of her difficulties. She attributed many of her struggles to her age, invoking it as a reason for some of her challenges.

Standardized tests have had an adverse impact on the educational opportunities for students of color.[7] Consequently, as we saw with Mr. Holmes, many of the most influential ideas about test bias deal with race. A conversation between Amade, Natalie, and Jasmine illustrates how complex and insidious some of these ideas can be. The three students were part of a larger group interview that took place the week after they sat to take their professional readiness exam. At one point in the interview, they discussed possible reasons for different performance levels across racial groups and the adverse impact of the exam. As African American women, they spoke about this topic mostly as it pertained to African American test-takers. (A group with a different racial identification might have focused the conversation differently.) Amade began by talking about getting up at 6:30 a.m. the week prior and riding with approximately 20 other African American test-takers from her program to take the exam at a nearby site.

> When we were all on the bus and going to take the exam, I was comfortable and relaxed. But when we actually got there and I saw how many Caucasian students were there, it was kind of intimidating because I didn't expect it to be majority Caucasian students. I expected us to be the majority. But we were the minority. And I was like, *OK*. It was kind of intimidating. It was like, *Wow, I don't think I'm gonna do as well as they are.* And they were sitting there, and they had their books and stuff all studying before. And I was like, *Wow, OK.*

At the testing site during this administration, there was indeed a visible mixture of test-takers in terms of race as well as age. Some of them had preparation books open to complete some last-minute studying as they waited to be admitted to test rooms. Amade and others observed that these students who were studying were white. I, too, made these observations as I entered the lobby with Amade and the rest of the students who were on the bus. Seeing the unexpected, mismatched racial balance and white students studying made Amade and others intimidated or nervous and think they were not going to do well. Other people in the interview agreed with Amade that they noticed and felt the same way to varying degrees.

Thinking about this situation, it is possible that any student, regardless of race, might feel nervous and less confident upon seeing other test-takers studying in this situation. During my younger years as an athlete, my nervousness before competition would always spike upon entering a place of competition and seeing other athletes warming up in their bright, colorful uniforms. They looked so prepared, so ready! Was I as prepared as they were? In this same way, any person could compare oneself to another person and subsequently question or change the appraisal of their own abilities. However, at least part of these effects upon Amade and others in the test was tied to ideas about race and standardized test performance. It wasn't just that there were other students in the lobby studying. There were *white* students studying. Their ideas were not tied to race in an abstract way but were connected to ideas about how much effort and preparation they thought African American students put forth compared to students of other races. The continuation of their exchange illustrates this second layer.

NATALIE: I do agree with them, but I think it's a lack of preparation. We don't really prepare ourselves to take it. We just say, *Oh let me go take this test* when like, we should've had our books too. So I think it's a lack of preparation.

JASMINE: I think it's lack of preparation because we don't study as much as everyone, like as much as we should. We just go in there unprepared and thinking we're gonna pass and get mad at the end when we know we failed because we didn't prepare.

NATALIE: People try to put you down – you get put down by like stereotypes and stuff if you let it. If you don't let it get to you, you will be fine. Everyone is just as smart as everyone else. I believe that we don't put as much effort and study time as other races do. And I learned that in class when my professor gave us statistics. But we don't, we really don't. And I think that if we did, our test scores could probably be a lot better. A lot better. I believe what Jasmine said, we use stuff like that as an excuse.

There's no excuse, we're just as smart as everyone else. We just have to put more effort into it.

There are many layers not only to this situation but to how the students make sense of it. We need to carefully unpack these layers to have a detailed understanding of it and to think productively about the ways we frame our own experiences with standardized test and licensure exams. We need to see the Big Assumptions and ghosts in the room.

Big Assumptions that Hold Us

In their book *How the Way We Talk Can Change the Way We Work*, Robert Kegan and Lisa Lahey distinguish between assumptions and Big Assumptions.[8] An assumption is Big if we take it as the truth rather than realize that it is an assumption we are making. Big Assumptions are "not so much the assumptions we have as they are the assumptions *that have us.*"[9] Since Big Assumptions have us and we take them as truth, it is often difficult to pinpoint and articulate them. We look *through* Big Assumptions, allowing them to shape how we see and make sense of the world around us, rather than look *at* Big Assumptions. Kegan and Lahey address this idea mostly with regard to how people broadly think about themselves, but the distinction is relevant to specific topics as well, such as licensure exams. Below are some of the other characteristics Kegan and Lahey outline for Big Assumptions that hold us.

- We produce them automatically, without intention or awareness.
- We hold them as truths.
- They create a sense of certainty, that your perspective is reality.
- They help hold together our interpretation of the world or specific phenomena.

One Big Assumption that held me for a long time was that people would think I was lazy if I was not the hardest working person on a sports team, in a school class, or in an academic department. The idea sounds ridiculous, I know. Big Assumptions often sound ridiculous when we pinpoint them and articulate them aloud. But, Big Assumptions are not built out of nowhere. There are often good reasons and real experiences over long periods of time for the Big Assumptions that hold us. I developed this Big Assumption from many years of competitive athletics, never being the "top" performer in any academic class, and other experiences. I internalized these experiences, and they manifested through a Big Assumption that I had to work harder than everyone else and that doing so would make me more valuable. Occasionally, there are some situations that make our Big Assumptions visible and apparent to us. These are crucial opportunities to alter thought patterns.

When Natalie and Jasmine reflected on their thought process upon entering the test center, it revealed some of their Big Assumptions about who prepares for standardized tests and who does not. In fact, we can see Natalie talking around and working through some of these Big Assumptions, stating that it isn't true ("Everyone is just as smart as everyone else") yet believing that "we don't put as much effort and study time as other races do." She starts to develop some psychological space between herself and her Big Assumptions, which is crucial "to move them from subject to object, where we can look at them, turn them around in our hands, and consider altering them."[10] We'll return to Big Assumptions below.

Ghosts in the Room

There are Big Assumptions holding Natalie and friends in the exchange above, but there are also ghosts in the room. Of course, I am not referring to literal apparitions haunting them at the test site but something else not too different. Social psychologist Claude Steele uses this term, "ghosts in the room," to describe the presence of stereotypes and other judgments in a given social setting.[11] A more technical term for this is *identity contingency:* "possible judgements, stereotypes, opportunities, restrictions, and treatments that are tied to one's social identity in a given setting."[12] These ghosts in the room can be positive and negative, and they can relate to people's race, gender, professional occupation, sexual orientation, age, and other identity markers. We experience these ghosts in subtle and salient ways. While taking the comprehensive exams for my doctoral program, a ghost in the room dealing with my age popped right up and terrorized me. While trying to make sense of the statistical gibberish on my computer screen (recall the story from Chapter 1), I felt every comment, look, and interaction with other classmates – about my age – stack up on top of me. Under this weight, I felt what an epic failure it would seem to everyone and myself if I failed the exam. These scenes started to play out in my head as I tried to regroup. A specific part of my identity and ideas associated with it increased the affective load of the situation. Steele's phrase "ghosts in the room" gets at the invisibility of these ideas and how they may lurk and haunt us in certain situations. Steele also pinpoints why identity contingencies matter to people in situations.

> The problem is that the pressure to disprove a stereotype changes what you are *about* in a situation. It gives you an additional task. In addition to learning new skills, knowledge, and ways of thinking in a schooling situation . . . you are trying to slay a ghost in the room, the negative stereotype and its allegations about you and your group.[13]

To be clear, Steele is not talking about when people believe a negative stereotype about themselves or hold them as Big Assumptions. He is talking about the presence of possibility. Steele's use of the word *allegation* is also important. Allegations about us – even ones that are false and that we do not believe – can still affect us. One does not have to believe a negative identity contingency for it to shape their subjective experience of a situation. I did not believe my age marked me as different from any other student in my doctoral program, but I understood that classmates thought it marked me as different. The possibility of me disconfirming (or confirming) other people's ideas weighed upon me in that pressure situation, adding an additional layer to my affective load as I attempted to disprove it or simply tried not to be bogged down by it.

The group's idea about how much different races prepare themselves for standardized tests is also a ghost in the room. It is a specific idea about a social identity group to which they belong (a racial group) in a particular situation. Seeing white test-takers studying in the lobby triggered this ghost to appear. Ghosts in the room do not only concern African American test-takers, of course. These ghosts can be connected to many different social identities in a particular situation. For Tammy, entering a test center and seeing students who appeared much younger than her might trigger the ghost in the room about her age and feelings of unpreparedness for standardized tests. A testing facility on an elite, wealthy campus might trigger a ghost in the room for a student who comes from a lower-income background and has had this label "stuck" on them for some time. There are ghosts in the room about gender and performance on certain academic subjects as well.

The Effects of Big Assumptions and Ghosts in the Room

What are the effects of Big Assumptions and ghosts in the room? We can see some of the effects by taking a more detailed look at the setting the students described. To recall, seeing white students studying in the test center lobby is what triggered the ghost in the room about Black test-takers not preparing themselves for standardized exams. We might even say that the Big Assumption about who studies and who does not primed the group to see this ghost in the room.

There are crucial details to this scene, however, not captured by the description offered by Amade and friends. They saw only part of the scene. Prior to entering the test site, some of Amade's classmates (all of whom were African American) also had been studying during the bus ride to the site. This is a detail I noticed as I rode the university bus with students to the testing center. They used the 30-minute ride to the test center for a final study and review session. Contrary to Natalie's claim that "we should have had our books too," some of her classmates also brought preparation materials to study during the break between tests. They *did* have their books too! Furthermore, not all of the white students in the test center lobby had materials and were studying. In fact, surveying the lobby, I saw only a few of the many white students there studying.

These additional details paint a fuller, more accurate picture of the scene. It was not one of white students with their noses in books diligently preparing for this exam and Black students showing up unprepared. In the test center lobby, there was a visible mix of Black and white students. Some students in each group brought study materials and were using them. Most students, no matter how they appeared racially or ethnically, were just there waiting for the exam to start, and looking groggy on this early Saturday morning.

The fuller details of this scene raise some important questions. Why did Amade and friends miss these other details that could have given them more affirming messages about their preparation that day? These details were objective, concrete, and right in front of them. Were they simply looking in wrong direction? Did they blink at the wrong time? The answer to these questions, of course, is no. The Big Assumptions they held functioned as a selective filter that highlighted only the details that would confirm the Big Assumptions.

A analogy to the medical field helps here. There is a real medical condition called agnosia. This condition is often the result of trauma, such as a brain injury. People living with agnosia lack the ability to process information from a specific sense. There is no impairment with regard to taking information in through sight, sound, and other senses. But the ability to process this information is impaired. A person with visual agnosia would see a thin, shiny silver object about the size of a pencil with three or four prongs at the end, but they would not be able to recognize the object as the fork that it is.

Amade and friends do not have the medical condition of agnosia. But the Big Assumption about Black test-takers works in a similar way. It filtered what they were able to process. Functionally, it clouded their ability to process disconfirming evidence: that there were some Black students studying and some white students not studying. This point leads to some concrete actions to take against it, and I will return to this point in the application and extension portion after this chapter. But first, we must dig a bit deeper to where these ideas come from.

The Origins of Big Assumptions and Ghosts in the Room

If Big Assumptions and ghosts in the room are influential on what people see and how they experience a situation, it's important to understand where they come from. These ideas have histories – biographies, so to speak – and come from somewhere. We get a clue to where some of these ideas and experiences come from when we realize that the current generation of new teachers is the most tested generation of students in the history of American public education. Particularly since the No Child Left Behind act of 2001, standardized tests have been a consistent thread woven through their educational lives: to assess state standards, for admission into specialized and magnet schools, for college admissions, and more. This oversaturation of high-stakes and standardized tests creates many opportunities for students to be socialized to feel certain ways about them. You probably don't need research to prove this point; you know it from experience.

For Amade and the students at the center of this chapter, their prior experiences with standardized tests influenced how they experienced their licensure exam. In other words, the Big Assumptions that clouded what they could and could not see did not come out of nowhere. A host of test-related experience over the course of their educational lives, some of which were very painful, helped create them.

Kendrice opened up to the group about her earlier experiences with high-stakes, standardized tests and how they influenced her feelings about teacher licensure exams. As a middle schooler in New York City, she was selected to take the Specialized High School Exam, a test that selects students for magnet and themed high schools with that designation. Students have to be selected to take the exam, and then admission to the special schools depends upon their scores. Kendrice noted that she was one of only five Black students that she saw taking the exam the morning it was offered. The rest appeared to be white or Asian. Her recollection was that on testing day, "Everybody else was like, *Oh, these Asians are better than me*" and bought into stereotypes about Asian American students and academic performance. She resisted this deficit thinking of herself, noting that she wasn't "brought up to think that way." Her thought process at the time was, "I'm going to ace this no matter what anybody says."

After the test, students were gathered around talking about their experiences on the exam and excitedly asking one another which answers they picked on certain questions. Kendrice narrated the scene like this:

> Afterwards, everybody grouped up with their friends like, *Oh, what you got for this answer?* And I knew some of the people, but didn't know them personally, from playing against them in sports. And there was this one group that was like, *Oh, what'd you get for this answer?* But they were kind of loud. But I was just standing there waiting for my friends to come out from their test. And they were like, *What you got for answer number 5?* And one girl said, *It doesn't matter, she failed anyway.* Come to find out, I got higher than her. But she got into the high school and I didn't.

This comment hurt Kendrice. When she saw her mother at home, she told her about the comment and that she didn't want to continue education. Her mother counseled her, "Don't let people depict on what you want to do in your future. You have to do you." Despite her mother's encouraging words, the comment stayed with Kendrice: "It really hit me hard where I kind of didn't care what I got but just went with the flow."

Kendrice spoke about this personal experience alongside the topic of test bias and how stereotypes factor into the exam and people's experiences with the exam. Her point in sharing this scene from middle school was to illustrate that some people, like her, actively resisted stereotypes about themselves. She knew the ideas were not true. After all, she aced the test in middle school. But still, these ghosts in the room stayed with her into her young adult years. She said the idea still crosses her mind when thinking about the licensure exam, but she knew "If I really put my mind to it, I can do it."

Natalie's experience serves as another example of how prior encounters with other standardized tests can shape how a student experiences their licensure exam. Natalie discussed her experiences with an Asian American classmate in elementary school and how Natalie and her classmates assumed the student was smarter than all of them because she was Asian American. "That's what I used to think all through elementary school when we had to take standardized tests and stuff," she recalled. "I used to just always think she was going to do better than me, so I didn't really try my best on the test."[14] Looking back on the experience, Natalie knew that she and her classmates were buying into a racist stereotype that Asian American students were naturally gifted at academics and test-taking. This belief (part of the Model Minority Myth) still persists today.[15] Recalling more details about the experience, she noted that her Asian American classmate used to ask Natalie and her friends for help on homework and for answers. The pattern continued to where Natalie and her friends gave the student fake phone numbers so that she couldn't call them at home any more. In Natalie's recollection, the student didn't make the honor roll. "But everyone thought that she was so much smarter than us when she really wasn't," she summarized. "Now I know better, but as a child, everyone was like *Oh, because she got an A on the first test, she's so much smarter than us. And she really wasn't.*"

Natalie looked back on these experiences differently, but they still filtered into how she experienced her licensure exam. She relayed a story from the exam she took the previous week where she was talking with another test-taker as they were packing up their materials right after the exam.

> I was sitting next to a girl and she was an Asian girl, and we were talking while we were packing up pencils and stuff. And I told her, *Yeah, this is my first time taking it and I'm not good at math so I know I'm gonna fail.* And she was like, *Oh yeah, you're probably gonna fail.*

Incredulous at this response (and laughing while retelling it to the group), Natalie narrated her internal monologue at the time: "How you gonna tell me I'm gonna fail?! You can't tell me that! You can't tell me that! It really just hit me that she said that!" The comment continued echoing through her thoughts even a few minutes later in the exam room: "She really just said I was gonna fail!"

In narrating this scene, Natalie was clear to note the other student's racial appearance, that she was Asian American, specifically, like her classmate from elementary school. Like Kendrice, Natalie did not believe these stereotypes to be true. Recall her comment from earlier in the chapter that "everyone is just as smart as everyone else." Yet, this ghost in the room about race and standardized test achievement was not far from her testing experience.

Understanding Experiences Holistically

We have seen so far in this chapter how Big Assumptions and ghosts in the room can affect people in testing situations. They affect people by shaping what evidence they see, influencing their interpretation of this evidence, and then reinforcing the Big Assumptions and ghosts in the room. Figure 4.1 illustrates this cycle.

We can see in this figure how prior experiences give way to Big Assumptions and ghosts in the room. These, then, shape the selective evidence we see or do not see. All evidence is subject to interpretation, and we may interpret evidence in narrow ways. These narrow interpretations then reinforce our Big Assumptions and ghosts in the room. Figure 4.2 illustrates this cycle with some specific examples from Natalie and her group in this chapter. Look closely at these two figures to understand how it represents this cycle.

This cycle has the potential to lock people into a closed loop of thinking. Consequently, it's important to think about opportunities to exit from this cycle. Are there ways to see different evidence? Are there ways to understand the origins of Big Assumptions and ghosts? Figure 4.3

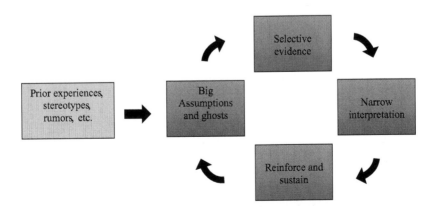

Figure 4.1   Big Assumptions and Ghosts in the Room Cycle

Source: Author.

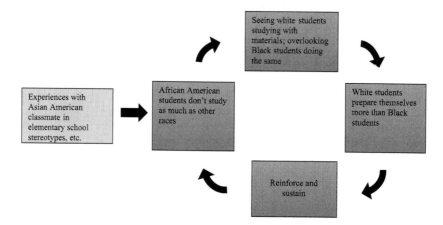

Figure 4.2   Big Assumptions and Ghosts in the Room Cycle with Content
Source: Author.

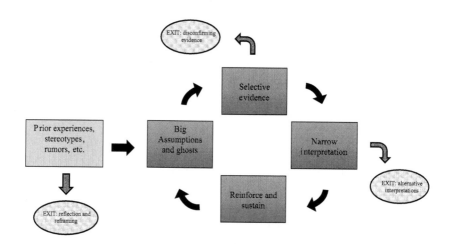

Figure 4.3   Big Assumptions and Ghosts in the Room Cycle with Exits
Source: Author.

introduces three potential exits from this cycle. These exits are 1) discon-firming evidence, 2) alternate interpretations, and 3) reflection and refram-ing of prior experiences.

Finally, Figure 4.4 fills in these exits with examples relevant to Natalie and friends, based upon the contents of this chapter. In this final figure, we

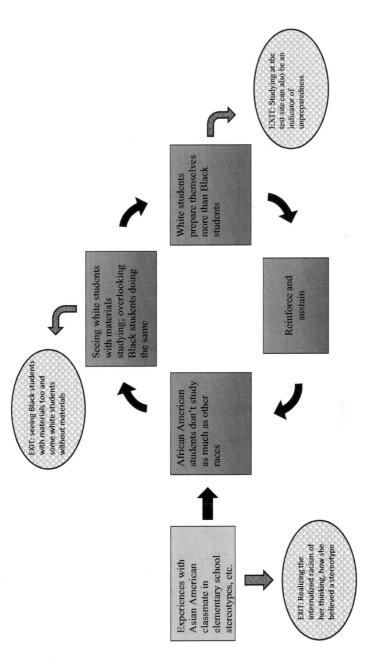

Figure 4.4 Big Assumptions and Ghosts in the Room Exits with Content

Source: Author.

get an idea about what might move Natalie out of the cycle built around Big Assumptions and ghosts in the room.

The application and extension that follows this chapter picks up from these figures. The exercises will lead you through filling in these categories for yourself and thinking about exits. While doing so, the goal is *not* to convince yourself that the Big Assumptions are entirely false or that you have been deceiving yourself all along. Big Assumptions have histories and don't dismiss that easily. The goal is to build "psychological space" between yourself and your Big Assumption "to move them from subject to object, where we can look at them, turn them around in our hands, and consider altering them."[16] Natalie and other students in this chapter were on the cusp of building this necessary psychological space, but they weren't quite there. With this space, we no longer look through the Big Assumptions, allowing them to shape how we make sense of ourselves and the world around us; we look *at* the Big Assumptions and make them into lowercase assumptions. The result of this process is that we are able to build qualifications, caveats, and exceptions around our assumptions.[17] You'll look to achieve these results in the application and extension.

Application and Extension: Scaring Away the Ghosts in the Room

This application and extension builds upon some of the ideas in Chapter 4. Specifically, it focuses on identifying and reframing Big Assumptions and ghosts in the room. These two processes – identifying and reframing – make up the two exercises and their steps below. The figures at the end of this chapter are important springboards for this application and extension, so revisiting them and keeping them in mind as you progress through the following material will be beneficial.

Exercise 1: Understanding the Inner Wheel

The inner cycle of Figure 4.4 represents a pattern through which people make sense of themselves with respect to licensure exams. Table 4.1 at the end of these application and extension sections has adapted the boxes of that figure into columns. Exercise 1 leads you through the three steps of filling out these columns. Understanding these steps alone is only a first step toward reframing ideas of cultural bias. Exercise 2 helps push past these ideas and reframe them.

Table 4.1 Identifying Ghosts and Big Assumptions

Big Assumptions, ghosts, and you	Roots and sources	Selective evidence	Disconfirming evidence	Interpretation	Alternative interpretations

Step 1: Big Assumptions, Ghosts, and You

In order to reconfigure Big Assumptions and beat back ghosts in the room, we first have to identify them. This process is not exactly easy since we often take Big Assumptions as truth: we look through them and not at them. Trying to identify a Big Assumption is a bit like a fish trying to notice water. It has been taken for granted for so long that pinpointing it can be difficult. Similarly, identifying ghosts in the room can be difficult because they only appear in certain circumstances.

We can start identifying Big Assumptions and ghosts in the room by thinking about *salient aspects of your identity in context with licensure exams.* Here, I refer to aspects of your identity that matter when it comes to the world of testing. For Tammy, it was her age. Being older was a salient part of her identity; it mattered when it came to math and testing. For Amade, Natalie, and Jasmine, being African American mattered. It came into play when they thought about some testing situations and how much African Americans prepare for tests (or so they thought). For me in graduate school, it was my age – or being the youngest one – and how I felt people overestimated my intelligence. The key question is this: What are the Big Assumptions and ghosts in the room for you in the world of licensure exams, and what specific aspects of your identity are they connected to? Fill in this information in the column "Big Assumptions, ghosts, and you."

The point in thinking about these questions, at least initially, is not change these Big Assumptions or believe that the ghosts in the room are fake. The simple act of identifying them doesn't necessarily make them go away. The point early on is to study Big Assumptions and ghosts in the room and to develop a better understanding of how they work. In what kinds of situations do they show up? What are the key elements of these situations? Is it in certain locations or places? Or among certain groups of people? When they do show up, how do they affect you? Do they make you freeze up? Try less? Or try extra hard and overperform? Once again, the idea in these initial steps isn't to dismiss the Big Assumptions or ghosts in the room. The point is to understand them better and know how they work in your life. Consider these questions as you fill out the first column.

Step 2: Selective Evidence

Selective evidence is what supports Big Assumptions and ghosts in the room. We observe interactions and situations according to our particular standpoints. Thinking back through this chapter, Natalie and friends saw evidence as they entered the test center that supported their assumption that African American test-takers do not prepare themselves as much as test-takers of other races. This observation was some white students studying. We can never take in all the information about a situation. All observations are limited and partial, even if they are meaningful to us. In the "Selective Evidence" column of Table 4.1, think about what you have observed, heard, noticed, etc. that has supported your Big Assumptions or ghosts in the room. Put this information in that column.

Step 3: Interpretation

Information, facts, and observations do not interpret themselves. We interpret them according to our experiences, cultural standpoints, and more. One teacher sees a student dozing off in class and interprets it as evidence of the student's disinterest in school. Another makes this same observation and interprets it as evidence that the student is tired. The same observation is subject to different interpretation. The "Interpretation" column of the table pushes you to make explicit and visible the interpretations you have made or continue to make from the evidence in Step 2.

Exercise 2: Exits and Interventions

The three steps of Exercise 1 led you to identify information and thoughts of the inner wheel of how people make sense of licensure exams. Exercise 2 leads you through the important steps of identifying exits and interventions to these steps. Exits and interventions are specific places where you can step outside of this inner cycle, generate new thinking patterns, and develop more useful ways of sense-making.

Exit 1: Roots and Sources of Big Assumptions and Ghosts

Big Assumptions and ghosts in the room have histories. Each of them started somewhere. For Kendrice, these ideas could be traced to her earlier experiences with the exams and hurtful, racist comments made toward her. Natalie absorbed these ideas from prior educational experiences with an Asian American classmate and from a professor who promoted deficit stereotypes. For Ashley, the idea came from a well-meaning staff person on campus, Mr. Holmes. Where did these ideas come from for you? The term *excavate* is relevant to the process of tracing where these ideas came from. When archaeologists excavate a site, they dig through many layers of rock and earth in order to find what it is they are looking for. Before using remote sensing techniques like radar, archaeologists would more often find unexpected items while excavating a site.

You might find unexpected memories and feelings while tracing and digging up the roots of your Big Assumptions and ghosts in the room. However, without tracing their roots, we are left at their mercy. Tracing where they came from – understanding their biography, so to speak – starts to give us agency to deconstruct and dismiss them. Give some thought to the roots and sources of your Big Assumptions and ghosts in the first column. Put these ideas in the "Roots and Sources" column.

Exit 2: Disconfirming Evidence

The "Selective Evidence" column of Exercise 1 focused on observations that support Big Assumptions and ghosts in the room. As the title suggests, all evidence is selective and limited. Regardless, we have the ability to actively seek out evidence that challenges or disconfirms our deeper assumptions. Thinking back to Natalie and friends at the test center, they could have actively sought out disconfirming evidence in this situation. Are there African American students with study materials with them as well? Are there white students who are not studying? As noted in this chapter, the answer to both of these questions is yes. Think about disconfirming evidence you have seen that challenges or calls into question your Big Assumptions or ghosts in the room. Put this evidence in the corresponding column.

In some instances, you might conclude that you haven't seen any such disconfirming evidence. Tammy might have made this conclusion if she had completed this exercise: she hadn't seen any students of her age who had passed the exam. If this is the case for you, complete this part by imagining what real and meaningful disconfirming evidence would be. In Tammy's case, meaningful disconfirming evidence would have been examples of real people her age who had passed the exam. Perhaps examples of people who had struggled to pass the exam (like her) and then passed (like Heather, Shonda, and Destiny) would also serve as disconfirming evidence that some people are simply born good standardized test-takers. Think about what meaningful disconfirming evidence would be, and put it in this column. Identifying what this evidence would be puts you in a position to actively seek it out.

Exit 3: Alternative Interpretations

While seeking disconfirming evidence is one way to alter assumptions, this process does not erase the existing evidence in front of you. Let's think back to Natalie and friends in the test center lobby. While looking for disconfirming evidence, they could not make the white students who were studying disappear. As I noted in Exercise 1, information, observations, and data of all types are subject to different interpretations. We can be active in trying to develop interpretations – alternative interpretations – that are healthy for us, boost our confidence, and challenge unhelpful Big Assumptions that hold us. For example, one could interpret the scene in the test center much differently than Natalie and friends did. One could look at the students who were studying in the lobby before the exam as *less* prepared and trying to desperately cram in some final effort before the start of the exam. Similarly, one could look at students who were not studying as poised, prepared, and ready for the exam. These are not radical stretches of logic. They are justified interpretations with different effects upon students. The point of entertaining alternative interpretations is to avoid narrow interpretations that only serve to validate Big Assumptions and trigger ghosts in the room.

Take this approach and apply it to the "Alternative Interpretation" column. Look at the interpretations you have in the "Interpretations" column, how those are connected to the "Evidence" column, and develop some reasonable alternative interpretations of this evidence. This exit may be the most difficult of all since our interpretations are often limited by our own experiences and cultural standpoints. They are *our* interpretations for reasons. Having a conversation with someone else and letting them into this thinking exercise can be a way of developing alternative interpretations as well, since doing so expands beyond your own patterns of sense-making.

Notes

1 Christine I. Bennett, Lynn M. McWhorter, and John A. Kuykendall, "Will I Ever Teach? Latino and African American Students' Perspectives on PRAXIS I," *American Educational Research Journal* 43, no. 3 (2006): 531–75.

2 Daniel Koretz, *Measuring Up: What Educational Testing Really Tells Us* (Cambridge, MA: Harvard University Press, 2008).

3 Ibid.

4 Ibid.

5 Barnard Weiner, *An Attributional Theory of Motivation and Emotion* (New York, NY: Springer, 1986).

6 Albert Bandura, *Self-Efficacy: The Exercise of Self Control* (New York, NY: Worth Publishers, 1997); Weiner, *An Attributional Theory of Motivation and Emotion.*

7 Michael T. Nettles et al., "Performance and Passing Rate Differences of African American and White Prospective Teachers on PRAXIS Examinations" (Princeton, NJ: Educational Testing Service, 2011); Nicholas Lemann, *The Big Test: The Secret History of the American Meritocracy,* 1st edition (New York, NY: Farrar, Straus and Giroux, 2000).

8 Robert Kegan and Lisa Laskow Lahey, *How the Way We Talk Can Change the Way We Work: Seven Languages for Transformation* (San Francisco, CA: Jossey Bass, 2001).

9 Kegan and Lahey, *How the Way We Talk Can Change the Way We Work,* 68.

10 Ibid, 85–6.

11 Claude M. Steele, *Whistling Vivaldi: How Stereotypes Affect Us and What We Can Do* (New York, NY: Norton, 2010).

12 Valerie Purdie-Vaughns et al., "Social Identity Contingencies: How Diversity Cues Signal Threat or Safety for African Americans in Mainstream Institutions," *Journal of Personality and Social Psychology* 94, no. 4 (2008): 615–30.

13 Steele, *Whistling Vivaldi,* 111.

14 We might also think about Natalie's response here as a protective one. Putting forth less effort (i.e., undereffort ing) can be a way to protect oneself from feeling bad about poor performance. The thinking goes that the poor performance is a product of undereffort ing (a conscious decision) rather than a lack of skills displayed through much effort.

15 Here we might also think about how the situation from the standpoint of Natalie's Asian American classmate. How could her actions be responses to stereotype threats and identity contingencies she was experiencing from Natalie and other students? See Wayne Au and Benji Chang, "You're Asian, How Could You Fail Math? Unmasking the Myth of the Model Minority," *Rethinking Schools,* 2007, http://rethinkingschools.aidcvt.com/archive/22_02/math222.shtml

16 Kegan and Lahey, *How the Way We Talk Can Change the Way We Work,* 85–6.

17 Ibid.

The Story of How We Feel   **5**

Understanding the Emotional Side of Licensure Exams

Emotions can be a slippery topic of discussion. In western society, people frequently think emotions are "lesser" than thoughts. If a person is emotional (the logic goes), then they are not thinking clearly or reasonably. In fact, accusing a person of "just being emotional" is a well-worn tactic to dismiss another person's experience or perspective on an issue. The truth of the matter is that feelings, emotions, and affective states often come before thoughts. We *feel* the impact of a situation before we sort out our thoughts about it. Even further, affective states like being nervous or anxious can temporarily inhibit focus, memory, and other skills needed to do well in an evaluative situation. The same goes for licensure exams. People's emotional states leading up to and during the test are important.

Given the importance of emotions, one of the first activities I would regularly do with the students in this project was to generate words that come to mind when we think about the licensure exam. We would list these words on a big sticky note taped to the wall and use them as a starting-point of discussion. Later, we would do the same for words that describe how we felt while actually taking the exam. The word cloud in Figure 5.1 is a collection of these words students generated. The size of each word represents how often it was cited by students – bigger words more often, smaller words less often.

Looking at this word cloud, think about which of these emotions you've experienced in context with a licensure exam. Considering the relationship between emotions and tests, it may be tempting to associate

Figure 5.1   Emotions Associated with Teacher Licensure Exams

negative feelings like "nervous" with failing and positive feelings like "confident" with passing. Without a doubt, certain negative emotions like anxiety and fear can interfere with functions that people need to perform well in performance situations.[1] Most people have experienced this phenomenon in some capacity: if you are nervous or anxious, your mind races and you find it more difficult to concentrate on the task at hand. You think about the consequences of not doing well, rather than what is right in front of you. Perhaps it takes longer to complete the task at hand, which usually isn't good in a timed testing situation. However, it would be simplistic and inaccurate to make a direct association between these emotions and passing or failing. There are certainly instances of people working through anxiety and other negative emotions in order to perform well on tasks, whether those tasks are academic, athletic, or something else. Recall Destiny's story from Chapter 2. She felt the *most* nervous the time she finally passed the exam. Even in instances when negative emotions might work out to lower a person's score (perhaps they take longer on the exam and have to guess on the last ten questions), this lower score does not always equate to failing. People who experience anxiousness and fear can still perform well on tasks before them. On the other side of this situation, experiencing positive emotions like confidence does not automatically lead to passing. Plenty of people leave an exam feeling confident about their performance only to be surprised and disappointed when they later see the results. Given the importance and complexity of emotions, we need some core concepts to help us understand them.

Stress, Emotions, and Coping

Psychologists have been studying stress and how people respond to it since the 1950s. As with any topic that has received so much attention, stress has been studied from a variety of perspectives. One useful perspective focuses on the person and their relationship to the stressors they encounter in their environment.[2] But what is "stress"?

At a basic level, stress is a stimulus that gets in the way of a person's wellbeing: our health, comfort, and stability – emotionally, physically, and otherwise.[3] Oftentimes, stressful stimuli come in the form of events. These events can be large-scale and happen on a worldwide scale, such as the threat of a terrorist attack, or the events can be small-scale and happen only in your personal life, such as encountering a traffic jam on your way to work that is sure to make you late. A test, such as a teacher licensure exam, can also be a stressor that interferes with a person's wellbeing, especially their emotional wellbeing. Each of these events calls upon our human facilities in order to continue healthy functioning.

Appraisal: How We Make Sense of Challenges

Another key element to stress is *appraisal*, or the continual evaluations of this stress in our environment and how it might pose a challenge to our wellbeing. People make hundreds of appraisals in different situations each day. Many of these appraisals are made quickly and without much deliberation or pensive thought: when it is safe to make a left-hand turn into oncoming traffic, how to confront a person in your social circle about something hurtful they said, or if it's necessary to apply sunblock on a sunny day. Each of these situations requires a judgment about the potential impact of the situation on our wellbeing, whether that impact is a car accident, losing a friend, or having sunburn for a week. We typically make appraisals like these without too much deliberation and thought. Finally, appraisals vary from person to person. Two people might make different appraisals from the same potentially stressful stimuli in their environment. That friend of yours who drives much faster than you do and makes close-call left-hand turns? They appraise the risks associated with driving differently than you do.

With some stressors, we appraise the situation once, act, and then move past the stressor. Other stressors that we encounter, like an upcoming exam, initiate ongoing and more complicated appraisals. In encounters like these, we do not appraise the situation once and then act, as we might while making a left-hand turn into traffic: *it's safe for me to make the turn . . . now*. Rather, appraisal is ongoing. We continually take in more information about the situation and continue to evaluate its potential impact on our wellbeing. This kind of ongoing appraisal is more common with licensure exams. Although this ongoing process is complex, two different categories of appraisal are helpful thinking tools: threats and challenge.[4] When we appraise a situation to be a threat, we perceive it to jeopardize our wellbeing. It may harm us emotionally, physically, or in another manner. We might feel a pit in our stomach, tightness in our chest, or dizzying anxiety in the presence of a threat. A bit differently, we may appraise a situation to be a challenge. As a challenge, it may be difficult, but we understand that it may also be beneficial to us because it stretches us to grow. Instead of a pit in the stomach, we might feel some butterflies that give us useful nervous energy.

A simple athletic example can illustrate: an athlete in a weight room might attempt to bench press a weight that is at the threshold of their strength. This encounter may be appraised as a threat: failing to bench press the weight may cause embarrassment, a sense of failure, and possibly injury. In response to this appraisal, the athlete may feel fear. At the same time, the athlete likely knows that tests at the threshold of one's strength are precisely what enables one to become stronger. Consequently, the athlete also appraises the encounter to be a challenge that holds the potential for gain and growth. Licensure exams can function in the same way. Although you may experience them as a threat, at the same time, you can see them as holding the possibility for professional growth and learning.

Coping: What We Do to Reduce Stress

A final and important concept associated with stress is coping. Coping is what we do in the midst of stressful events and stimuli in order to make do. More specifically, coping is what people do to reduce, minimize, or tolerate stress when they encounter situations that tax their resources. By taking actions to cope, we typically try to manage/alter the situation that is causing us stress and/or regulate the emotional aspect of our encounter with the situation. Coping entails cognitive efforts (thinking and making sense of situations in different ways) and behavioral efforts (taking specific actions in situations). These efforts are not fixed during stressful situations but instead are constantly changing. Like driving a car on a winding road, our coping strategies change as does the terrain. A concise psychological definition of coping is this: "constantly changing cognitive and behavioral efforts to manage specific external and/or internal demands that are appraised as taxing or exceeding the resources of the person."[5]

A final point with coping: all coping isn't good coping. We use coping strategies to manage or reduce the stress and demands of a situation. Reducing the stress and demands of a situation does not necessarily promote successful performance on the task at the heart of the stressful encounter. In other words, a person may effectively *manage* the stress of a situation through a coping action, but this same coping action may *reduce or sabotage* their chance at success. While driving from Point A to Point B on that winding road, you may press the brake pedal to slow down your car and better navigate the terrain. This action reduces the stress of the drive, but it does not support the larger goal of arriving at Point B on time. Similarly, a person may cope with the emotional stress of an exam by avoiding preparation activities or convincing themselves that the event isn't important. Avoiding these activities reduces the emotional stress of the upcoming exam, but this same coping act might undermine the person's overall goal of performing well. All coping isn't good coping. Contrast this coping approach with one that reduces the stress of a situation by engaging in preparation activities. This point about coping is critical for understanding our own actions, the reasons behind them, and how they affect our larger goals.

The Story of Our Emotions

Stress, appraisal, and how we cope are key elements of the emotional side of exams. But there is an additional aspect that deals with the story we build around our experiences. A great deal of thought from psychologists, linguists, and other scholars has considered the stories that people develop from their life experiences and how we build a sense of self and identity from these stories. Scholars have been interested not simply in these stories but also in the tone of the stories and the stories *underneath* the stories. In his book *The Stories We Live By: Personal Myths and the Making of the Self*, Dan McAdams argues that if we want to understand ourselves, we must understand what he calls *the narrative of the self*: "the personal myth – that I have tacitly, even unconsciously, composed over the course of my years. It is a story I continue to revise, and tell to myself (and sometimes others) as I go on living."[6]

By using the term *myth,* a narrative perspective does not mean that we are deceiving ourselves or not facing reality, as the phrase "that's just a myth" might suggest. The term also doesn't mean we are comparing ourselves to Zeus, Apollo, or other Greek gods. Like Greek myths, however, the term points to our tendency for creating stories to "bring together the different parts of ourselves and our lives into a purposeful and convincing whole."[7] As we will see throughout this chapter, the narratives we make do not always have happy endings or portray ourselves positively. The point is that the myths we compose bring different parts of ourselves together and do so through the same narrative qualities in any compelling movie, show, book, or story:

- Beginnings, middles, and ends
- Conflicts and resolutions
- Elements of plot
- Protagonists
- Causes and effects

Digging a bit deeper, narratives also have different tones to them based upon the selective content of the story and how it is told.[8] A person who experiences hardships in life can narrate these experiences through an optimistic tone and genuine hope that things will get better. You might know people like this: despite the bad luck they encounter, they remain hopeful moving forward in life. Another person with identical experiences could narrate the events in a pessimistic tone: their lot in life is only misfortune. There are different ways to narrate the same experience. These different tones can be a result of our childhood experiences, the models that were around us, and more. Sometimes understanding our experiences through optimistic tones helps us to cope with challenges.[9]

Thinking beyond narrative tone, there are a number of narrative templates that we draw from in order to structure our myths. These templates guide the kind of protagonist at the center of the action, the tone, and if the narrative ends in harmony, chaos, victory, or something else. These templates do not determine what we think. Rather, they are specific types of narratives we have been exposed to over the course of our lives, and we draw from these without much conscious thought to compose our experiences into narratives. Table 5.1 outlines four common templates in context with narrative tones.

As noted in this table, pessimistic narratives tend to draw from tragedy and irony. Optimistic narratives tend to draw from comedy

Table 5.1   Four Narrative Templates

Narrative templates	Tone	Plots	Hero	Central message
Comic	Optimistic	People finding happiness and stability by minimizing obstacles and constraints.	Ordinary, common person.	We all have opportunities to find happiness and to avoid pain. We can seek happy endings for the stories we live.
Romantic	Optimistic	Excitement, adventure, and conquest in a dangerous journey full of changing obstacles.	An exceptional person: bolder, wiser, or more virtuous than the rest.	We encounter great challenges in life, but we can win and become more enlightened if we stay vigilant.
Tragic	Pessimistic	Heroes falling from grace, sacrificing themselves, and being separated from the natural order.	An exceptional, extraordinary person with a tragic downfall that results in their eventual ruin.	We encounter pain, pleasure, happiness, and sadness. The world is not to be trusted because the best intentions can lead to ruin.
Ironic	Pessimistic	Stories of triumph or chaos where a person attempts to sort out the ambiguities and puzzles the world presents.	Ordinary, common person.	We encounter ambiguities and confusions in life that are beyond our capacities to solve. We are not promised victory.

Adopted from Dan P. McAdams, *The Stories We Live By: Personal Myths and the Making of the Self* (New York, NY: Guilford Press, 1993), 51–2.

and romance.[10] Note too that comic myths are not necessarily funny, and romantic myths do not have to deal with love. From a narrative stance, these terms have different meanings than they do in most of our daily conversations. Our lives and the narratives we make never fit a single one of these templates. Rather, we draw from all of these templates in different ways to narrate ourselves.[11] These templates, the stories underneath the stories, are tools we use to create an identity and build coherency out of our scattered experiences – ones we've had and ones we are yet to have.

Narrating our lives is also a way of coping with the uncertain or difficult experiences. Even if what is happening in our lives is not what we desire, we still craft it into a coherent narrative to understand it. We see this play out in tragic ways around abuse and self-blame. In order to make sense of abuse, sometimes survivors blame themselves – as if they are at fault for the abuse they endured. Though inaccurate (a person is never at fault for abuse they endure), this narrative form is a way to make sense, cope, and have some perception of control over the situation. Ultimately, it is through this intersection of emotions, stress, coping, and narratives that we will learn from the students' experiences below.

How People Cope and Narrate Their Experiences

The sections that follow introduce three new students: Keyon, Brandon, and Rose. We'll use the ideas about coping and narratives as tools to understand their experiences with licensure exams and standardized tests more broadly. As in the previous chapters, this deep dive will help us work through the application and extension exercises that follow this chapter.

Keyon

Confidence can be deceiving, especially in challenges that bring stress. We have the skill to reflect upon how we feel and our affective states, but sometimes this reflection is objectively false or self-deceiving. There are layers of experience and meaning we stack upon one another in order to make sense of experiences. Keyon, who we'll meet now, helps us to understand this point.

Whoopty-Doo, Just Another Test

Keyon described his mentality going into the exam as "not scared at all."
While other students might have been uncertain or scared, Keyon felt that
he wasn't. The second year elementary education major unpacked this
perspective in our group interview as students were discussing their initial
feelings about the exam after having taken it the previous week:

> Going into this whole exam I wasn't scared at all. I think because I
> was listening to certain people and they were like, *Don't be scared;*
> *there's nothing to be scared about.* And I knew from past experience
> that there was nothing to be scared about. So I went in there like I'm
> just taking another test, whoopty-doo.

Of note in Keyon's description is a reference to the members of the advice
network around him and their messages to not be scared. Keyon suggested
that he took these ideas on as his own and that he wasn't scared. The past
experience he refers to is taking the SAT three times in high school and
receiving about the same relatively low score each time. From these
experiences, he knew there was "nothing to be scared about." He
emphasized his low-key emotional approach to the exam with the somewhat sarcastic idiom "whoopty-doo."

Although Keyon represented himself as unafraid of the exam, later in
the group interview, as other students opened up about their fear and
intimidation of the exam, Keyon revealed a different side of his emotional
experience with the exam. He voiced his concern about making mistakes
while taking the exam.

> I was just thinking hard during the whole process because I didn't
> want to – maybe that's why I messed up – because I didn't want to
> mess up. I don't know. I didn't want it to be like a trick question. I
> was really thinking hard on these answers and on these questions
> they were asking and what answer I was gonna put down.

We can see from this excerpt that Keyon was focused on the idea of
"thinking hard" while taking the exam because he didn't want to "mess
up." His concern about messing up was connected to a suspicion that
there might be "trick questions." Although he didn't unpack what a trick
question might be, oftentimes people associate this idea with multiple
choice questions and the suspicion that some answers might be there to

mislead test-takers. These concerns about trick questions and thinking hard during the exam suggest that he took it a bit more seriously than he initially said.

Keyon admitted that he did not prepare much for the exam. The little preparation that he did engage in was centered on an abstract idea of "strategies." Talking about traveling with other students to the exam, he referenced being "on the bus looking through the study book, just going over strategies in my mind." Talking more about his mindset during the exam, he noted he was "determined that I was going to do well after I started seeing some strategies that I was using during the text." For Keyon, it seems that preparing for the exam meant knowing strategies to crack its code rather than focusing on content that might be covered. Doing well on it meant applying those strategies (like eliminating multiple choice answers) during the exam. If we think about Keyon's concern about trick questions, it makes sense that he would focus on strategies designed to keep him from being tricked.

As the group conversation got deeper and students talked more about their emotional experiences with the exam, Keyon's stance continued to evolve beyond the unaffected, unbothered one he initially took up at the start of the interview. He described his stance like this:

> I just get real intimidated with tests. Like when I sit down to take a test, I just feel like the test is thinking *I own you.* That's how I look at it, *You're gonna listen to me. Walk the way I tell you to walk.* That's how I feel. It's bad that I feel that way.

Keyon's statement is a startling reversal from the position he took at the start of the group conversation when he said the test was no big deal, "whoopty-doo." In his narration, Keyon went from being not scared at all, to "thinking real hard" so that he wouldn't be tricked, to getting "real intimidated." Ultimately, in Keyon's construction of this story, the test has agency, telling him, "I own you."

How should we make sense of Keyon's reversals? Was Keyon lying at the start of the interview about his perspective and emotional state? The answer is no. Keyon wasn't lying. He was coping. Looking at Keyon's experience from the perspective of stress and coping renders a much different reading. When Keyon called the exam "just another test" and added "whoopty-doo" for sarcastic emphasis, he was using a specific coping strategy: minimizing the importance of the stressful event in order to lessen its pressure. This strategy is similar to an athlete telling herself that the championship game she is about to play in is "just another game" when it is certainly not just another game. From a coping standpoint, lessening the importance of the championship game is a strategy to avoid feeling extra pressure so that the athlete can perform at the same level she does during regular games. In Keyon's case, there is much evidence of his emotional distress: his preoccupation with trick questions, "really thinking hard," and his feeling like the test owned him. It follows that he would use some kind of coping strategy to lessen the emotional stress leading up to the exam. But once again, all coping isn't good coping. His coping strategy did little to prepare him for the exam. In fact, lessening of the test's importance seems to have driven him away from intentional preparation activities.

From "Whoopty-Doo" To "I Own You"

Looking at Keyon's experience from a narrative perspective also provides an illuminating rereading. Agency, or who has it, is a key element in narratives. We learn this point in elementary grammar when studying the difference between subjects and objects: subjects in sentences have agency; they *do* the verbs. Objects in sentences do not have agency; they *receive* the actions. Keyon's narration begins with him in full control of the action and endowed with agency. Consider the language he uses:

- "I wasn't scared . . ."
- "I knew from past experience . . ."
- "I went in there . . ."
- "I'm just taking . . ."

In each of these stems, Keyon located himself as the one in control, the one with agency, the one doing the action. His emerging narrative takes on an optimistic tone with comic features. As noted above, comic does not mean funny in this sense. Rather, Keyon's laid-back attitude helps minimize obstacles in front of him, a feature of the comic template. Later in his retelling of the experience, Keyon opens up the possibility of the test having certain qualities (trick questions) that might present difficulties to him. The test is still an object in this part of his narrative, and Keyon is still the one with agency and in control. But, the test is now a particular *kind* of object, one that poses problems, difficulties, and obstacles to Keyon's success.

By the end of Keyon's narrative, a dramatic shift has occurred between who or what has agency and who or what is an object. The test is no longer a passive object but has become a subject – almost like a person – with agency. Keyon personifies the exam by giving it human qualities: the exam can think, talk to Keyon, make demands of him, and make a claim of ownership over him. Consider the language Keyon uses at the end of his narrative to represent the exam and what it says to him:

- "I own you."
- "You're gonna listen to me."
- "Walk the way I tell you to walk."

In endowing the test with agency, Keyon is no longer the author or protagonist in his narrative. In fact, the narrative is no longer his. He has given it over to the exam, and Keyon has become an object in the exam's narrative. Instead of thinking about the test, the test is thinking about Keyon. Instead of talking about the test, the test is talking about Keyon and making antagonistic demands of him. Keyon knows that his thinking pattern is unhealthy ("It's bad I feel that way"), yet he can't escape it. By losing control of the narrative, it moves from an optimistic comedy about reducing obstacles to a pessimistic tragedy about downfall and ruin. Thinking about the pessimistic tone of Keyon's narrative, it should come as no surprise that he felt helpless. We feel helpless when we perceive ourselves to be in situations where we have no control, no agency.

This narrative view of Keyon's experience further explains the coping strategy that he used. To recall, he minimized the importance of the exam as a way to reduce its threat to his emotional wellbeing. Minimizing the importance of the exam was an attempt to not feel the test say "I own you. You're gonna listen to me."

Brandon

Keyon illustrated some of the ways coping might sabotage success and the complicated narratives that a person can build around fear. This recognition is important to have a level-headed view of our actions and their outcomes. Similar actions, however, can have different outcomes if situated within a different plan of preparation and organized by someone else. Brandon, who follows, teaches us some of these lessons by staying grounded in who he is and building an unexpected narrative around his experiences.

That's Not How I Do Things

Like Keyon, Brandon's preparation for the exam was informed in part by his prior experience with other standardized tests like the SAT. While in high school in New Jersey, he had a group of friends who all planned on going to college. This meant that taking and doing well on the SAT was a large concern for them since so much emphasis was put on this exam. Little by little, as Brandon remembered it, these friends started "dropping like flies." When it came time for the SAT, only Brandon and one of his friends were left. Despite many of Brandon's friends not taking the SAT, he had a generally positive experience with standardized tests, scoring advanced proficient in reading and writing in high school.

When it came to the teacher licensure exam, like Keyon, Brandon also tried to make a distinction between himself and the other people around him, especially as it related to other people's anxieties and thoughts about performance. He summarized his stance like this:

> I was in a mind state where I was like, *Well, just because you had trouble with it doesn't mean I am.* It wasn't like I felt like I was higher up than anybody, it was just, *Because it didn't work out for you doesn't mean it's going to be the same for me.* What works for somebody might not work for somebody else.

Separating himself from other people specifically played into how much preparation Brandon put into the exam – or rather, how much preparation he did *not* put in. "You wanna study your brains out and everything like that," Brandon said, speaking not to specific classmates but in general, "That's not me. That's not how I do things."

Brandon's statement about "how he does things" was rooted in coping with the potential stress of the exam as it approached. His coping came into focus as he further unpacked this statement and how he saw himself as different from other classmates:

> I was kind of training myself actually for it not to be such a big deal. I think in total I may have studied for like three minutes. My whole thing about this whole test was just to be relaxed. It made no sense for me to go outside of my character.

By making reference to his character, Brandon was alluding to a general approach that he takes to stressful situations like high-stakes tests. "That's just how I am," he explained in reference to his approach. "I always say to myself, *All this time I could spend stressing out over it, I could really just be doing something more productive.*"

Brandon's approach to coping with the stress of the exam revolved around two actions: First, he distinguished himself from the people around him who were anxious about their performance. This move protected him from making a negative comparison, and it also preserved his belief in his own abilities. Second, he took action that would follow from a belief that the exam is nothing to stress about. This action was not studying much. The thinking process goes that if the exam is truly no big deal, then a person wouldn't study much. Brandon took these actions as a way to "train" himself not to stress.

Reading Brandon's plan and coping actions closely, we can see they are potentially disastrous: preparing for a total of about three minutes is typically not a recipe for success. In fact, this part of Brandon's approach sounds similar to Keyon's. Both of them prepared little for the exam. However, it is important to see how Brandon's decision not to prepare himself extensively for the exam fit into a larger plan that he had. Brandon's plan was to take the exam in the unstressed state he was aiming for and see what result that produced. These results would then give him the information he needed to decide the right amount of effort to put in (and potential stress to experience) as he prepared to take the exam again, if needed. "If I get close to passing," he told himself, "That means I'll study a little bit more. If I was far away, I was going to study my ass off for it." We can see from these details that Brandon's avoidance of strenuous preparation was not *only* a coping strategy to manage feeling stressed. It was also a coping strategy about the exam and fit into his larger plan for success – something Keyon did not have. Fortunately for Brandon, he didn't need to execute any additional stages of his plan. He passed the exam on his first try.

As a secondary English major, Brandon was confident and strong in the reading portion of the exam. However, he knew the topics of the passages would be boring to him and that he needed to find a way to stay awake and engaged. "Alright," he told himself. "We gotta try to make these things as interesting as possible." In order to do this, Brandon imposed topics that were interesting to him over the boring topics in the exam passages.

> Like if it be about art or something, I would just change the concept. There was this one passage about some bugs, so I turned

it into some bugs in the NBA. I had to do something or otherwise I would have fell asleep.

This absurd image of some bugs playing in NBA was imaginative enough to keep Brandon awake and engaged on the reading exam. Instead of thinking about trick questions and strategies to avoid them like Keyon, Brandon came up with methods – even silly ones – to stay awake and engaged.

While Keyon was concerned with trick questions and a general notion of "strategies" during the exam, Brandon's approach was informed by technical knowledge of the exam and what he needed to pass. He was confident about passing reading and writing but said "there's no chance in hell I'm going to pass math." However, Brandon knew that there were two ways to pass the exam: by passing each test itself or by achieving a certain composite score from all three tests. By this second method of passing, Brandon knew that if his math score was low, points from his reading and writing could "carry over" and help. "Alright, I gotta do really good in reading and writing so I could help my math score," was how he planned.

On the math exam, Brandon surmised two points about the exam by listening to the advice and experiences around him. The first piece of information was that the test was a computer adaptive exam. This means that the questions get more difficult as one gets deeper into the exam. He came to this point from listening to the experiences of people around him. The other piece of information was that a person needed to get a little over half of the questions right to pass. He gathered this point from looking at the range of possible scores and the number of questions on the exam.[12] Based upon these two pieces of information, Brandon described his approach like this: "Alright, I gotta put all my energy and time into getting them first twenty questions right . . . If I get three more right, I'm good."

The Adventures of High-Stakes Tests

There are key difference between Brandon and Keyon at the level of coping. In a similar way, we can also see some key differences between the two at the level of narrative. While Keyon's narrative spun out of his control, Brandon's narrative did not. Brandon retained agency throughout his entire narrative and did not slowly give it over to the exam. In fact, details from Brandon's experience in the exam show how he attempted to impose his own will on it: imagining new scenarios onto the reading passages, using the design of the test to his advantage, and aiming for a composite score to pass.

Digging deeper, Brandon's narrative contains elements of a specific template: romance. This romance template does not mean Brandon's story is about love and the kind of passion we associate with romantic movies. From a narrative perspective, "romance celebrates the excitement of adventure and conquest."[13] Of course, this template (especially in movies) may include love and the pursuit of a romantic interest, but it can also be pursuit of many other adventures and conquests, as in Homer's *Odyssey* or an *Indiana Jones* film. Brandon's adventure and conquest is passing his licensure exam. Within this romantic framework, Brandon narrates himself as a kind of hero. By hero, I don't mean a character like Batman or Wonder Woman. In a romantic narrative sense, a hero is someone exceptional and different from the masses, one who "embarks on a perilous journey, overcomes great obstacles, and triumphs in the end ... someone who is bolder, wiser, or more virtuous than everybody else."[14]

Specific elements in Brandon's narrative follow this template. Consider how he sets up his experience. He began by distinguishing himself from those around him who were anxious and diligently preparing themselves: "because it didn't work out for you doesn't mean it's going to be the same for me." From the start, Brandon is "someone exceptional, different from the masses" – like most of our cinematic heroes: Frodo Baggins, Luke Skywalker, and Katniss Everdeen. Essential to this kind of hero's journey are challenges that one must navigate. Brandon sets up these challenges in his narration, especially on the math exam: "There's no chance in hell I'm going to pass math." His description creates drama; the odds are not in his favor. But, like all heroes, Brandon has a plan to succeed in the midst of this steep challenge and low odds. As we learned above, his plan included taking it under a low stakes setting first and then, if needed, "studying his ass off," and more.

Romantic heroes are "bolder and wiser" than the rest, and Brandon uses knowledge about the organization of math problems to plan his approach – like Luke Skywalker channeling The Force to shoot two proton torpedoes into the Death Star's reactor core. Even as Brandon narrates the fine details of the experience in the testing room, he attends to the obstacles he encountered and how he overcame them: the boring reading passages sure to make him fall asleep and his imaginative tactic to stay awake. Brandon's narrative communicates the message that shines through romantic narratives:

We embark on a long and difficult journey in life in which circum-stances constantly change and new challenges continually arise. We must keep challenging and moving if we are to win in the end. But we are confident that we will win.[15]

Rose

The cases of Keyon and Brandon might give the impression that people who fail the exam construct pessimistic narratives, and people who pass create optimistic, heroic ones. While some cases fit this pattern, narra-tives are not always so simple. As noted earlier in the chapter, people with similar sets of experiences can craft very different narrative myths and tones. Additionally, people do not draw from only one narrative template to story their lives. People often draw from a combination of different narrative templates to create compelling myths out of their experiences.[16]

Rose's narrative reflects these points. She is an important addition to Keyon and Brandon. We briefly met Rose in Chapter 3 through Destiny. Rose was one of the influential people in Destiny's network and, as a close friend, provided different kinds of information about the exam (advice, logistics, personal experiences, and more). You might recall that Destiny characterized Rose as listening to what other people said about the exam and not realizing that she is unique, her own person. We'll meet Rose on her own term in this final section of the chapter. Rose – how she copes and especially how she narrates her exam experiences – will keep us from drawing narrow conclusions from Keyon and Brandon.

Coping by Avoiding the Exam

The events that make up Rose's narrative closely parallel those of Tammy, who we learned about in previous chapters. Rose entered college set on becoming a teacher. Yet, she ultimately discontinued her pursuit of an education degree because she could not pass all parts of the licensure exam. She failed all portions of the exam the first time she took it, slowly bumped up her scores over time through much deliberate effort, and eventually passed the reading and writing but not the math. As was the case for Tammy, the clock was ticking against Rose. She eventually changed to a different major and watched Destiny and other friends continue on in the program. This decision was not an easy one for Rose.

Rose coped with the stress of the exam in similar ways to Keyon. The first time she went in to take it, she went in intentionally unprepared. She represented her thought process at the time like this: "Well, I'm not going to pass this test. It is what it is. I barely made it through the SATs. I got into college because of my GPA, so I'm not passing this exam." She grabbed some preparation materials from the campus study group but never opened them up before exam. She described her reason like this:

> Because I feel like the exam was like the SATs, and SATs you can't really practice for. So I just wanted to go take it, see what it's about, and if I don't pass, then I will know what I'm looking to study for. So took it, just went in there, did what I have to do, and that was it. Got my scores, didn't pass. I said, *Okay, now I have to buckle down because I need to pass.*

From the standpoint of stress and coping, there are three things at work in Rose's decision: 1) her belief that you can't practice for the exam, 2) her decision not to prepare, and 3) her intention to use this experience to practice in the future. If we take Rose's perspective seriously, we can see that there are some internal contradictions: If you can't practice for the exam, why would you go to see what it's like to then inform your practice for a retake? After Rose failed the exam, she committed herself to a rigorous preparation schedule, including paying $300 for a personal tutor between semesters. She did not simply go to take it again and try to get lucky – which would follow from a belief that you can't prepare for the exam. Rose's effort calls into question her stated belief that "you can't really practice" for the exam and her decision to go in blind. Why would she do this?

If you've been reading this chapter closely, you know the answer: coping. Rose heading into the exam unprepared "to see what it's about" was a way to protect herself from the emotional risk of failing. The protective thinking goes like this: *If I don't study for the exam and I fail, then I failed because I didn't prepare, not because of something about me.* Contrast this thinking with the steeper stakes for someone who fails after preparing a great deal. These kinds of failure experiences after much effort can damage confidence and beliefs about one's abilities.[17] The thinking goes like this: *I put in all this effort and still failed. There isn't much else to do.* In sum, Rose's decision to go into the exam was a coping tactic to lower the stakes of the exam. Coping mechanisms can make us play tricks on ourselves.

This approach to coping even shaped how Rose experienced questions on the exam that she didn't know. She recounted how those questions didn't have much of an effect on her, such as making her more nervous or anxious. Her thought process when encountering these questions was, "I'm going to fail anyway, so whatever. I'm sure this one's not going to make a difference out of the twenty-nine I just got wrong."

Not Failure but a New Beginning

Given the *events* of Rose's experience are similar to those of Keyon and Tammy, we might expect her to compose a pessimistic narrative that draws from tragic or ironic templates. However, she made sense of these events in radically different ways, composing these events into a narrative much different from that of Keyon and Tammy. In other words, it isn't just about the dots; it's also how you connect them and what color markers you use to do so.

Rose composed an optimistic comic myth. We often associate the term "comedy" with a movie genre and films that have funny plots that makes audiences laugh. Comic and comedy mean something different from a narrative standpoint: "It brings the sense that the world is starting afresh and that things will work out. Comic plots, whether funny or not, concern how people find happiness and stability in life by minimizing obstacles and constraints."[18] Central to Rose's optimistic narrative was her growing to differentiate herself from the people around her and carve out her own path forward. This differentiation – writing her own story – was related to both big and small events: from developing study methods that worked for her to deciding that the professional path so many others were taking would not work for her.

We can see evidence of this crucial change as Rose spoke about her shifting perspective on getting advice from other students about the exam. "The first time, I was like *How is it? Is it easy? Did you pass? How'd it go?*" she started off, recalling the questions she asked her friends. "I was always asking them like, *What is it about? How can I do this? How can I do that?*" Rose's aggressive approach to soliciting other people's perspectives inserted a chorus of voices into her narrative. She consumed herself with this chatter by comparing herself to other classmates. "If this person's passing, why can't I pass?" she would ask herself. The comparison would then continue to what they were learning in class and even the school system they attended:

Like, we're learning the same material. Some of us were in the same education classes. I even put New York in the category. Like, we were in New York together, the same New York schools. I'm not getting this like you are!

Over her months of studying, Rose came to think differently about the attention and feature roles she gave other students in her narrative. From the advice of some close friends and mentors, she slowed down to focus on herself: "You know what, I just need to focus on *my* thought process," she told herself.

Because I realized that I had a different thought process from everybody else and I needed to focus on that. So I didn't really want anybody saying, *Well you know, just go in there and knock it out.* Or like they were telling me in the beginning the first time I took it, *Just go in there, oh you got this.* No, you don't know what I'm going through, so I'm just going to come up with my own structure and do it my own way. I didn't really want anybody to interfere.

Rose applied this thinking not only to messages and advice from classmates but to tactics for approaching specific tasks on the exam. Rose provided a specific example from the timed essay, a task that caused her much trouble the first time she took the exam and during study sessions.

But the second time I took it, understanding that I had a different thought process, I knew that it was all about me. My confidence level really skyrocketed. I said, *Well, okay, this is what I understand. This is what I'm going to do, and that's how I have to deal with things. And this is how I have to write it.* Everybody could be sitting there, bombing out this essay, but I know I have to go: intro, body, and so forth to make it out. So, I really didn't worry about anybody. That really helped my confidence, understanding that I was different.

These details from Rose's narration are not about the ways she changed her approach to the exam. We can learn from these changes, of course, and many of them are similar to the changes Destiny and others made between failing and passing the exam in Chapter 2. What is important about Rose is how she moves these people and voices from the center of her story to the margins. By doing so, she narrates this story as her own. She connects the dots with herself in the middle.

The arc of Rose's comic myth culminated through the new beginning she saw at the end of this journey to pass the exam. She made this optimism clear while talking about her decision to leave the education major after getting her final set of scores on the exam and learning that she hadn't yet passed the math.

> I actually did not beat myself as much as I thought I was going to when I found out my scores. And that's for so many reasons. Because I worked my tail off and I didn't feel like I was really giving up. I didn't feel like, *Oh, I'm giving up on teaching. Forget it.* That's not what I'm doing. I'm just getting over this hurdle to find another way for me to do what I want to do 'cause this is not working for me. And there's so many other ways to accomplish my dreams. And this is not going to stop me.

We can see in this narration how Rose's decision is about minimizing the obstacles in front of her, a key characteristic of comic myths. She viewed the licensure exam as an obstacle – likely as she did all along – but as one that she could maneuver around by changing her major and finding another way to become an educator working with young people. Her narrative positioned her as the hero whose journey was not what she wanted at the start, but she comes to the end of it changed and fuller because of how she grew along the way:

> I did what I had to do for me and I thought I did pretty good. Coming from someone who didn't even crack a book open the first time, to someone who worked their tail off, I'm proud of myself, honestly.

Conclusion

These portraits of Keyon, Brandon, and Rose help us to understand the ways people cope with emotions such as stress and how they build stories around these experiences. The application and extension exercises that follow this chapter pick up on these ideas and help you to understand your own ways of coping and building narratives. Are you like Brandon and prone to seeing the exam not as a threat but as a challenge to be overcome with skill and wit that other people might not have? Or do you have tendencies like Keyon, coping with the exam to reduce the stress but simultaneously undermining chances at success? Ultimately, it is crucial to understand the ways you go about coping with stress related to teacher licensure exams, if these coping actions promote success, and the related narrative you tell yourself.

Application and Extension: Keeping Track of Coping and Remixing Narratives

Exercise 1: Keeping Track of Coping

The ways that Keyon, Brandon, and Rose coped with the stress of their exam raise important questions. One of these questions deals with how successfully coping with the stress of the exam can simultaneously undermine success on the exam. I'll phrase the question like this: how can our coping play tricks on us? The steps below help to answer this question and give alternatives.

Step 1: Capturing Your Coping

Coping is a way of reducing the stress of a situation – one that you are experiencing in a moment or one that is approaching on the horizon, like a licensure exam. We saw in this chapter a number of different ways students coped with the potential stress of licensure exams. Understanding the specific ways you cope with the stress of a licensure exam is an important foundation. Over the course of a few days, keep track of all the ways you cope with the potential stress of your licensure exam. Resist the urge to complete this process in one sitting. Instead, keep track over a few days by jotting notes and looking for patterns.

Remember, coping can be *actions and thinking patterns*. Actions might be studying, avoiding studying, searching out information from people online, talking about the exam in particular ways, and more. Thought patterns might be thinking the test is "no big deal," thinking it *is* a big deal, paying attention only to certain aspects of the exam, comparing it to other experiences you've had, and more. Pay attention to both actions and thought patterns. Use Table 5.2 to keep track of them in the first column; identify as least three actions and three thought patterns. Also pay attention to the context of that coping. How and where does it show up? Put this information in the second column of the table.

The point right now is *not* to change your coping methods. Just like with Big Assumptions and ghosts in the room, the point is to identify and understand them. Don't go on to Step 2 until you've completed Step 1.

Step 2: Analyzing Your Coping

The next step after capturing some of your coping methods is to analyze them. Copy your coping methods from Table 5.2 into the first column of Table 5.3 overleaf. Then give some thought to if the coping method has helped reduce stress. Put those reflections in the next column.

One consistent idea through Chapter 5 was that all coping isn't good coping. A coping method may reduce stress, but it may also sabotage your success on the exam, as was the case with Keyon. In the final column, consider if your coping methods are *good* coping. Do they promote success on the exam, or do they push you away from the exam? How so? Recall here that many coping methods, such as thinking that the exam is "no big deal," could be helpful or harmful. For Keyon, it was harmful; this pattern of

Table 5.2   Coping Actions and Thoughts

Coping action	Context: How and where does it show up?

Coping thought	Context: How and where does it show up?

Table 5.3   Analyzing Coping Actions and Thoughts

Coping action	Does it reduce stress? How?	Is this healthy coping? Does it promote success on the exam? How?
Coping thought	Does it reduce stress? How?	Is this healthy coping? Does it promote success on the exam? How?

thinking was a way to cover for his fear and lack of preparation. For Brandon, it was helpful; the pattern fit into the stressless approach he had taken to other standardized tests (with proven success) and fit into his larger plan for the exam. This final column will take the most sharp analysis of all.

What conclusions can you draw from the information in the right-hand column? In light of this information, what are your next steps? What coping methods should you keep, and which ones should you rethink? As a final note in this exercise, coping is not as simple as swapping out one activity for another. It is about understanding if your use of certain methods (both actions and ways of thinking) manages stress *and* promotes success on a challenge.

Exercise 2: Understanding the Story You Tell Yourself

Exercise 2 focuses on understanding how you narrate your experiences with standardized tests: the story you tell yourself about your experiences in this area. The following steps ask a certain level of thought and action from you. It might be tempting to skip around these steps and complete the lightest ones first. Resist this urge and complete them in the order outlined below.

Step 1: Surfacing Your Story

What specific words describe your past experiences with standardized tests? Take a few minutes to list these words or make a word cloud with them. After identifying these words, write a few paragraphs that explain your general experiences with standardized tests. Perhaps think about different standardized tests you have taken and how you feel about the experiences of taking them. Let the list of words you identified be starting points. If it's easier to get these thoughts out by speaking instead of writing, record a voice memo on your computer or phone of you talking freely to answer the question. If you opt for this approach, take some time afterwards and transcribe your verbal response into written text. You'll need this written copy in the steps below.

Step 2: Narrative Analysis

As an educator, I tell my students I'd never ask them to do something I wouldn't also do. The same goes for this exercise. Below is a short version of my own narrative in response to the prompt in Step 1. We'll use my narrative as the basis for analysis first.

> My experiences with standardized tests have been a bit nervous. Early on I didn't pay much attention to them, but then as I got older, they seemed to be everywhere and right between me and what I wanted to do next, like becoming a teacher, then moving to California to teach (another exam?!), grad school, etc. But ultimately I've been successful in passing when I needed to – doing what I needed to do. I've had a few bumps along the way like when I took my comprehensive exams in grad school, but I was always able to navigate it in the moment and come out on top.

Tables 5.4 and 5.5 overleaf focus on narrative tone myth templates – two big ideas from Chapter 5. These tables are abbreviated from the tables in Chapter 5. We'll use them as tools to analyze my narrative for evidence of tones and myth templates. Remember that a person's narrative seldom fits only one tone or template. Rather, different parts of our

Table 5.4   Narrative Tones and Evidence

Narrative tone	Evidence from my narrative	Analysis
Optimistic: focus on the good things that have happened or hope that things will improve in the absence of good things.	*Ultimately I've been successful in passing.* *I was always able to navigate it in the moment and come out on top.*	Seems optimistic to focus on passing. The word "ultimately" also seems to indicate some closure around success and that it's a focus. "Always able to" definitely focuses on success and not on challenges.
Pessimistic: focus on misfortunes, failures, and bad events, or the negative costs to good things.	*They seemed to be everywhere and right between what I wanted to do next.* *I've had a few bumps along the way.*	This language sets the tests up as a barrier and something that might hold me back. Small focus on challenges or "bumps."

narrative may be optimistic, and other parts may be pessimistic. Further, we often draw from multiple myth templates in our narratives – not only one.

In my analysis, my narrative is mostly optimistic with a few possible pessimistic elements. Once again, the point here isn't to edit out any pessimism. It is there for a reason. The point right now is simply to understand the narrative tones. What about you? Do you see any other evidence of optimistic or pessimistic tones in my narrative?

The next grid focuses on narrative templates. Below is the evidence I see for the four narrative templates in my narrative. Notice as well how I'm paying attention to images, metaphors, or key phrases in my narrative and what they might indicate about the deeper ways I imagine the exam and my relationship to it. The same goes for who has agency in the narrative: me, the text, or something or someone else.

Table 5.5 Narrative Templates and Evidence

Tone	Narrative template	Evidence from narrative	Analysis
Optimistic	Comic: Encountering challenges and getting around them without too much stress. Minimizes obstacles, not making them into too big of a deal, and feeling that things will probably work out.	Early on I didn't pay much attention to them.	This part seems to be minimizing obstacles, highlighting the fact that I wasn't focusing on the exams too much.
	Romantic: Encountering challenges head-on and using effort, skills, and wisdom to conquer them. Typically ends in growth, learning, and/or some kind of success.	But ultimately I've been successful in passing when I needed to – doing what I needed to do.	This phrase definitely puts me in the driver's seat by focusing on my own agency and what *I* did. "Passing when I needed to" also sets me up as someone who comes through in the clutch.
		I've had a few bumps along the way … but I was always able to navigate it in the moment and come out on top.	Calling challenges "bumps" seems to minimize them (opposed to calling them "hurdles" or "obstacles"). The word "navigate" sets me up as a kind of explorer trying to figure a way – bumps on the road I'm traveling? I'm really surprised at the phrase "come out on top." It definitely seems like a phrase used in athletic competitions, so it makes me think about how I may be drawing from my experiences in athletics to think about licensure exams.

(Continued)

Table 5.5 (Cont.)

Tone	Narrative template	Evidence from narrative	Analysis
Pessimistic	Tragic: Encountering challenges head-on yet failing to conquer and overcome them. One's effort, skill, and wisdom are not sufficient but actually lead to downfall and failure.	None	None
	Ironic: Challenges remain a puzzle whose answers are withheld. Confusion and struggle are constant, typically ending in failure and frustration.	*They seemed to be everywhere and right between me and what I wanted to do next.*	This phrase definitely puts the agency on the exam rather than on me. The exam is everywhere, like something that can jump out and grab you! The word "between" also set up the exam to keep me from something I want.

In my own analysis, my narrative draws mostly form a romantic template but also comic and ironic, though much less so. Notice how I'm thinking deeply about the images and phrases I've used. Give my narrative a close look in these regards as well. Do you see evidence of any other templates in my narrative?

Step 3: Analyzing Your Narrative

Tables 5.6 and 5.7 are the same grids for analysis of your own narrative. Use these grids as I did above to generate evidence and analysis for the narrative you wrote in Step 1. Just as I did, pay attention to metaphors, images, and particular phrasings in your narrative. Pay attention as well to who has agency in your narrative: you, the text, or something or someone else. The more you've written, the more evidence for tone and myth templates you'll find.

Steps 4: Remixing Narratives

As noted above, the most important take-away from this exercise is awareness: awareness of what tones and templates you are using to tell yourself a story about experiences with standardized tests and licensure

Table 5.6   Your Narrative Tones and Evidence

Narrative Tone	Evidence from your narrative	Analysis
Optimistic: focus on the good things that have happened or hope that things will improve in the absence of good things.		
Pessimistic: focus on misfortunes, failures, and bad events, or the negative costs to good things		

Table 5.7 Your Narrative Templates and Evidence

Tone	Narrative template	Evidence from your narrative	Analysis
Optimistic	Comic: Encountering challenges and getting around them without too much stress. Minimizes obstacles, not making them into too big of a deal, and feeling that things will probably work out.		
	Romantic: Encountering challenges head-on and using effort, skills, and wisdom to conquer them. Typically ends in growth, learning, and/or some kind of success.		
Pessimistic	Tragic: Encountering challenges head-on yet failing to conquer and overcome them. One's effort, skill, and wisdom are not sufficient but actually lead to downfall and failure.		
	Ironic: Challenges remain a puzzle whose answers are withheld. Confusion and struggle are constant, typically ending in failure and frustration.		

exams. This is what you've done in the above steps. Awareness alone does not change these narratives. If it were easy to change a pessimistic narrative into an optimistic one, few of us would have pessimistic tones. We would just eliminate that material or tone. It's not this simple, however.

A different and more realistic way to think about shifting the narratives is through the concept of remix. We might not be able to change the narrative, but we can remix it. Music producers use a massive mixing console to fine-tune and ultimately finish a song. The console looks like a giant table tilted slightly forward with buttons and volume levels arranged in vertical rows. The rows separate each instrument or sound into an individual track. This allows the producer to tweak and adjust the "levels" of each instrument or sound: turning the bass up, bringing the snare drum down, and other such moves to get the song just right.

We can think about remixing your narrative in the same way. Consider each of the tones and templates as levels that you can adjust. Some you can turn up a bit by adding additional detail, extending your thinking and explanation, thinking more deeply, or moving it to the front or end of your narrative. Others you can turn down by deemphasizing it, going into less detail, or moving it to the center of your narrative so it isn't the start or conclusion. Once again, the point is not to eliminate pessimism or attention to struggle. If they are part of your narrative (your song), they are there for a reason. The goal is to turn them up and down to appropriate levels that remix your narrative.

Take this thinking about turning levels up and down to write a remix of your narrative. Your goals is to turn up some of the optimistic tone and related templates (comic and romantic) and turn down the pessimistic ones if the exercises above have shown you they are too high. Remixing the narrative is not turning it into fiction. It should still resonate as true for you.

Notes

1 Isabelle Blanchette and Anne Richards, "The Influence of Affect on Higher Level Cognition: A Review of Research on Interpretation, Judgement, Decision Making and Reasoning," *Cognition and Emotion* 24, no. 4 (2010): 561–95; Barbara L. Fredrickson and Christine Branigan, "Positive Emotions Broaden the Scope of Attention and Thought-Action Repertoires," *Cognition & Emotion* 19, no. 3 (2005): 313–32.

2 Richard S. Lazarus and Susan Folkman, *Stress, Appraisal, and Coping* (New York, NY: Springer, 1984).

3 Ibid.

4 Ibid, 12.

5 Ibid, 114.

6 Dan P. McAdams, *The Stories We Live By: Personal Myths and the Making of the Self* (New York, NY: Guilford Press, 1993), 11.

7 Ibid, 12.

8 Ibid, 48.

9 Shelley E. Taylor, *Positive Illusions: Creating Self-Deception and the Healthy Mind* (New York, NY: Basic Books, 1991).

10 Dan P. McAdams, *The Stories We Live By: Personal Myths and the Making of the Self* (New York, NY: Guilford Press, 1993), 50–1.

11 Ibid, 51–2

12 It's hard to know if Brandon was exactly right in these calculations. Each question on a licensure exam is not necessarily valued the same in scoring. Uncertainty surrounds this issue because test companies typically do not share this information because tests are licensed products protected under U.S. copyright laws. They should share this information, however.

13 Dan P. McAdams, *The Stories We Live By: Personal Myths and the Making of the Self* (New York, NY: Guilford Press, 1993), 51.

14 Ibid, 51.

15 Ibid, 51.

16 Ibid, 50.

17 Albert Bandura, *Self-Efficacy: The Exercise of Self Control* (New York, NY: Worth Publishers, 1997).

18 Dan P. McAdams, *The Stories We Live By: Personal Myths and the Making of the Self* (New York, NY: Guilford Press, 1993), 51.

Part 3

How Faculty Members Can Support Preservice Teachers

From Screening Out to Building Up

6

Frameworks for Teacher Educators

Although I've written the previous chapters primarily for preservice teachers, this chapter turns toward teacher educators and outlines two frameworks for thinking about students' experiences with licensure exams and how we support them toward success. There are certainly some frameworks and theoretical stances evident through the previous chapters, but this chapter drills down into two specific framework and related concepts. These two frameworks are self-efficacy[1] and socio-cultural theory.[2] Although these theories have progressed over decades, they have seldom been applied to the topic of teacher licensure exams. Since my audience in this chapter is teacher educators and not pre-service teachers, I take liberty to unpack the theoretical concepts at work in these frameworks so that readers can consider the deeper processes at work. I trust this intellectual exercise is one teacher educators welcome. The specific recommendations I outline in the following chapter generate from these two frameworks. Attending to concepts in this chapter, however, will help teacher education readers develop or modify practices in their specific contexts that anchor to these solid scholarly concepts.

These conceptual tools should be understood in context with how licensure exams are intended to function in teacher education programs and the profession more broadly. Some key findings about these functions from existing scholarship are important here. Consequently, this chapter begins by addressing these functions and outlining some key findings from relevant scholarship. This background provides necessary context for teacher educators to make policy and practice decisions.

Screens and Signals

Licensure exams have two separate functions that are often conflated, mistaken, or overlooked. Separating between these two functions allows for a clearer understanding of the politics around the exams, their role in teacher education programs, and how to make program-level decisions. These two functions are screening and signaling.[3]

As screens, licensure exams – and minimum cut scores, to be precise – are supposed to prevent (or screen) underqualified or incompetent teachers from the teacher labor market. This screen may happen at the entry point to a teacher education program through a professional readiness or "basic skills" exam, or it may happen when candidates take their content area exam if they fail to earn a passing score. Of course, there are variations in the timing of this licensure exam screen depending on program design or a particular state's configuration, especially with post-baccalaureate certification programs. Other professions such as law and medicine also have screens.

A signal is a bit different. In this function, licensure exams scores are supposed to predict (or signal) teacher effectiveness, most often through student learning in K-12 schools. In this policy logic, a licensure exam score indicates aspects of a teacher (e.g., content knowledge, pedagogical content knowledge, etc.) that will translate to student learning once the teacher enters a classroom. The exam score signals something to us now about what will happen (or not happen) in the future. A district administrator who considers a teacher's licensure exam score in a hiring decision is operating upon a signal logic.

All teacher education programs screen-out potential teachers through some mechanisms. GPA requirements, admissions essays, dispositions assessments, and more also serve to screen-out candidates and applicants. Screens, of course, are necessary because – ideally – they keep unqualified candidates from classrooms. Certain policies and practices of teacher education programs, however, can exacerbate screens, like tightening the threads of a web so less and less material can get through. These policies and practices are often entrenched, normalized, and unexamined. Programs whose primary function is to screen are different from programs that, in addition to screening, also build-up candidates so they can be successful. Minority-serving institutions, especially Historically Black Colleges and Universities and Tribal Colleges and Universities, have developed many of the most effective build-up approaches.[4] Table 6.1 distinguishes between screen-out and build-up approaches with respect to licensure exams. Of course, no program fits only one of these descriptions.

Table 6.1   Screen-Out and Build-Up Characteristics

Screen-out	Build-up
Presumes equity in previous stages of education system; deficiencies in student knowledge and skills are the result of individual efforts.	Presumes inequity in previous stages of education systems, expects deficiencies will manifest in student preparation levels, regardless of individual efforts.
Outsources remediation and support to departments or entities separate from teacher education program or department.	Shares responsibility for remediation and support; works in tandem with other departments or entities at institution.
Remediation and support costs students time and money (courses, credit hours, preparation materials, etc.).	Remediation and support minimizes costs to students (workshops within existing courses or outside of courses, preparation materials provided, etc.).
Makes no financial investment in student support.	Makes financial investment in student support (e.g., purchasing support materials, subsidizing exam cost, organizing and providing transportation to exam, etc.).
Students must fit into supports; supports unable to change as students develop.	Supports are built around student needs; supports adapt and change as students develop.
Single opportunity for growth.	Multiple opportunities for growth.
Decentralized remediation and support that isolates students from peers; "you're on your own."	Centralized remediation and support that strengthens relationships with peers; "lift as we climb."
Has non-certification path for students to finish education degree.	Has "soft landings" for students to transfer into other degrees from education.
Most contact with faculty members comes only after students pass a licensure exam and are admitted into education program.	Contact with faculty members comes as students are preparing for a licensure exam and after they pass.

Source: Author.

But, teacher educators should identify aspects of their program that fit screen-out models and consider how they might adopt build-up practices. Chapter 7, building upon the frameworks below, outlines many specific practices.

Scholarship on teacher licensure exams pivots around the ability of teacher licensure exams to act as appropriate screens and signals. Extending back decades, this body of work encompasses historical accounts of the National Teacher Exam (the precursor to the Praxis Series of exams), quantitative studies focused on candidates' scores, qualitative studies of candidates' experiences taking the exams, critiques of cultural and racial bias in the exams, and more. In the sections that follow, I briefly outline three findings from this body of scholarship around screens and signals. I focus on these findings because, as a group, they help push beyond two polarized, incomplete perspectives on the topic: that licensure exams are unnecessary (and culturally-biased) hurdles that only screen-out qualified candidates, or that licensure exams provide straightforward and meaningful information about teacher candidates. The truth of the matter from scholarship, I argue, is more complex than these available positions. Teacher educators should make policy decisions and plan for action in their own contexts with knowledge of the findings below, particularly if they commit to increasing the racial diversity of the teaching profession.

Impacts on Candidates of Color

One finding from quantitative studies in this area is that teacher licensure exams have an adverse impact on the opportunities afforded to preservice teachers of color. Michael Nettles and colleagues at Educational Testing Service illustrated this point dramatically in their 2011 report that focused on pass rates among African American and white first-time test-takers between 2005 and 2009 in the 28 states that used the Praxis series of exams.[5] The researchers focused on these two groups due to small sample sizes for other ethnic groups of test-takers. Table 6.2 illustrates first-time pass rates on the Praxis I exam for these groups.

The researchers also explored the relationship that other variables such as undergraduate, GPA, and institutional selectivity, had to passing Praxis I. Their analysis revealed that having a high GPA and attending a selective college or university were associated with higher exam scores, and being an African American student and being an education

Table 6.2   First-Time Praxis I Pass Rates Percentages, 2005–2008

	Reading	Writing	Math
African American	40.7	44.2	36.8
White	81.5	79.5	78.2

Source: Michael T. Nettles et al., *Performance and Passing Rate Differences of African American and White Prospective Teachers on PRAXIS Examinations* (Princeton, NJ, 2011).

major (opposed to majoring in a secondary teaching discipline) were associated with lower exam scores.

This adverse impact is not only a function of contemporary licensure exams but also goes back to their precursor, the National Teacher Exam. This exam and the phenomenon of teacher testing more broadly started in the south and spread to other regions during the mid-20th century. In South Carolina (an early adopter of this practice), the exam screened out approximately 3% of teacher candidates at Black colleges and less than 1% of candidates from white colleges in the 1967–1968 academic year.[6] South Carolina legislators raised the certification requirements of the exam two years later in order to increase the standards and rigor of teachers in the state. This new standard screened out approximately 41% of candidates from Black colleges and, still, fewer than 1% of candidates from white colleges.[7] The adverse impact that arbitrarily raising cutoff scores has on candidates of color is not only a thing of the past. Scholars argue against this quick-fix today because of the adverse impact it would have on teacher candidates of color and other negative outcomes to teacher quality.[8]

Since these findings deal with the Praxis I exam (an entrance require-ment for many programs), they hold important insight for understanding the prevailing whiteness of teacher education programs and the profession more broadly. If teacher educators – particularly at historically and predominately white institutions – wonder why their program remains overwhelmingly white, they cannot simply examine the students admitted into the program. Their analysis and support work must go back one step further to the pool of students, prior to admission, who are being screened out. Teacher educators should consider professional readiness exams as a crucial site of support, in addition to recruiting candidates of color with stronger academic profiles.[9]

All Struggles Aren't the Same

Another important finding from licensure exam research deals with how accurately professional readiness exams signal who will be successful further along in the teacher education program and the profession more broadly. Covered briefly in Chapter 2, a study by Drew Gitomer and colleagues at Educational Testing Service shed important light on this issue.[10] Gitomer and colleagues explored the relationship between success on Praxis I and success on Praxis II exams between 1999 and 2005. They looked at three groups with different levels of success on Praxis I – those who passed on their first try, those who passed after multiple attempts, and those who never passed – and how these three groups performed on Praxis II exams. Table 6.3 summarizes some results from their study, including the results disaggregated by African American and white test-takers.

Three aspects of the findings are important here. First, the results indicate that both African American and white preservice teachers who pass the Praxis I exam on their first attempt also pass later Praxis II exams with very high rates. In other words, there is little evidence of any major African American-white pass gap on Praxis II exams at this level, with the secondary math content area exam being one exception. Second, students in both racial groups who struggle to pass Praxis I also struggle to pass Praxis II. This finding means that the Praxis I exam, for some, serves as a useful signal for licensure exam success later in programs. Some students screened out of programs by Praxis I would continue to struggle and not successfully complete if admitted.

Third, all struggle isn't the same. Key differences along racial lines exist when students struggle with Praxis I. Both African American and white students who struggled to pass Praxis I and/or had low GPAs also experienced more difficulty passing Praxis II. However, the pass rate decline on Praxis II was significantly *steeper* for African American test-takers when they struggled to pass the exam. Data in the group differences column on the table illustrate this trend; the group differences increase under each Praxis II exam as students struggle to pass relevant Praxis I exams, yet this increase is greater for African American test-takers. This third finding indicates a crucial point: the consequences of struggling to pass a professional readiness exam or poor academic preparation, are greater for African American test-takers compared to white test-takers. Stated another way, whiteness and various forms of benefit associated with it insulate white test-takers from some of the consequences of struggling to pass Praxis I or poor academic performance. This trend is most pronounced on the Praxis II math exam where "race is the largest single predictor of licensure exam performance."[11]

Table 6.3 Praxis I and Praxis II Group Comparisons

	Elementary Praxis II Pass Rate		
	African American	White	Group differences
Pass Praxis I math on first attempt	96%	98%	2%
Pass 2+ attempts	86%	93%	7%
Did not pass	71%	86%	15%
	English Praxis II Pass Rate		
Pass Praxis I writing on first attempt	89%	96%	7%
Pass 2+ attempts	60%	82%	22%
Did not pass	44%	71%	27%
	Math Praxis II Pass Rate		
Pass Praxis I writing on first attempt	53%	86%	33%
Pass 2+ attempts	"half as much"	66%	30%
Did not pass	*	*	
	Social Studies Praxis II Pass Rate		
Pass Praxis I writing on first attempt	85%	93%	8%
Pass 2+ attempts	45%	67%	22%
Did not pass	44%	66%	22%

Source: Author.
Note: * = not reported.

For teacher educators, these results emphasize a few points. First, students who pass a professional readiness exam through multiple chances are more likely to need additional supports to pass their later content area exams. Second, for some students, being screened out of a teacher education program early on (and counseled to another major) saves them from spending precious time and money in a program that they will not complete. Of course, the balance between counseling students out at early stages and giving them necessary supports to take the exam "just one more time" is delicate. Third, how does being white (and the benefits associated with it) insulate white students from some of the toll that struggle takes on African American students?

This final point is crucial. Tentative answers come from a few different angles. Phillip Uri Treisman's classic study of college student math achievement found that the key difference in math achievement among racial groups was not motivation, academic preparation, time spent studying, or other factors. It was *how* they went about studying.[12] African American students diligently studied as individuals, shutting themselves off from insight, support, and feedback from their peers. Chinese students also studied diligently but collectively, connecting themselves with rich resources from their peers. Discussing the results of this study, Claude Steele noted that one response to stereotypes and identity contingencies for minoritized students (see Chapter 4) is turning in on oneself and away from supports, particularly if students of color are in predominantly white learning spaces. The absence of these identity contingencies for white students means supports are more readily available to them compared to racially minoritized students.

We can also look at this question from the angle of faculty members and the supports they provide students. We must consider the possibility that white faculty members, who comprise the majority of teacher education faculty, more frequently help white students. This pattern would follow not from the accusation that white teacher educators are consciously racist but rather because they might gravitate toward same-race mentoring relationship with students or believe that faculty of color are more "equipped" to support students of color. The quantitative results of Gitomer's study above require us to ask these uncomfortable questions.

Differences in How Exams Signal Teacher Effectiveness

A series of studies conducted with data from North Carolina illustrates the relationship between candidates' scores on licensure exams and other measures of teacher effectiveness, such as their students' scores on standardized exams. North Carolina is a frequent site of such studies because its database allows for matching between students and teachers over time, among other characteristics. Charles Clotfelter and colleagues at Duke University studied the relationship between a number of teacher variables (including Praxis II licensure exam performance) and fifth grade student achievement in North Carolina during the 2000–2001 school year.[13] The researchers found that one standard deviation increase in licensure exam performance predicted an increase in student math achievement by 1% to 2% of a standard deviation. To put this figure in context, this difference (an effect size) is negligible and of little practical impact on student achievement.

A series of studies by Dan Goldhaber reinforces the positive yet small relationship between licensure exam scores and student achievement. In one study, Goldhaber looked at the relationship between teacher performance on Praxis II licensure exams and elementary student achievement from 1994 to 2004 in North Carolina.[14] Goldhaber found that higher licensure exam performance positively related to student performance. However, the strength of the relationship varied depending upon the specific licensure exam a teacher took and by the subject matter (math or reading) in which students were tested. More specifically, Goldhaber found that "teachers who pass the test produce, on average, student achievement gains that are in the range of 3 to 6 percent of a standard deviation higher (in math) than teachers who fail."[15] As in the above study, this is a negligible difference in standard deviation.

Since the relationship between licensure exam performance and student achievement is not particularly strong, Goldhaber concluded that the exams, as signals of teacher effectiveness, produce many false positives (candidates who perform well on licensure exams but are not effective teachers) and false negatives (candidates who would have been effective teachers but are screened out of the profession by the exam). Simply raising cutoff scores, consequently, is not a neat solution to improving teacher quality because, among other effects, it would eliminate many effective teachers from the profession.

One final study led by Goldhaber highlights how licensure exams vary by race and gender in their ability to signal teacher effectiveness.[16] Using the same data in North Carolina, Goldhaber and colleagues explored the relationship between teachers' Praxis II licensure exam performance and elementary student achievement in reading and math standardized tests. The research team also explored questions about racial and gender match among teachers and students, and how these matches relate to student achievement.

The research team found evidence that as a screening device, Praxis II exams are effective at screening out poor-quality teachers from the profession. However, this screening function depends upon subject area. The exams function as good screens only for effectiveness in math and not in reading. With regard to signaling, as in other studies, performance on licensure exams has a positive yet small relationship to student achievement. However, the picture isn't quite this straightforward. Different Praxis II licensure exams have different levels of predictive validity – that is, the exam's ability to signal something accurate about teacher effectiveness. Further, this predictive validity is inconsistent across teacher race and gender. The exam's function to signal teacher effectiveness changes depending upon the race and gender of the teacher taking the exam. Finally, the drawback that a low licensure exam score has on student achievement can be mitigated by other factors, such as racial match between Black teachers and students of color. This important point is worth quoting for precision:

> Black and other minority students appear to benefit from being matched with a Black teacher regardless of how well or poorly that teacher performed on the Praxis test, and these positive effects due to matching with Black teachers are comparable in magnitude to having the highest-performing White teachers in the classroom.[17]

These findings reinforce take-aways outlined above, such as the inadequacy of simply increasing cutoff scores as a lever to increase teacher quality. The findings also reveal one additional take-away for teacher educators. There are other teacher characteristics that can balance out and, in some cases, supersede the drawbacks signaled by a low licensure exam score. The assets associated with racial and ethnic identity – working in context with other variables – are some of these characteristics. We lack rich understanding of these variables in context, but these findings illustrate that teacher education programs cannot rely on licensure exam scores alone to signal who will be an effective teacher.

Two Frameworks for Promising Practice

Teacher educators should take practical steps at both programmatic and classroom levels to support candidates as they progress through licensure exams. These steps should be grounded in concepts and frameworks about learning. Below, I outline two of these frameworks that are seldom brought to bear on this topic. Table 6.4 outlines some key points from these frameworks, both of which help move past simplistic stances on support that start and end with students only studying.

Self-Efficacy: Beliefs About Capabilities and Thinking You Can

Self-efficacy is a concept that refers to people's beliefs about their capabilities in specific areas. Outlining the construct in a foundational 1977 article, Albert Bandura argued that cognitive psychologists must examine the "efficacy expectations" that people hold about their capabilities rather than only examine the outcomes that people expect from their behaviors.[18] As this line of research progressed, self-efficacy became defined as "belief in one's capabilities to organize and execute the course of action required to produce given attainments."[19] Self-efficacy is not a general construct such as confidence or self-esteem that is unrelated to a specific domain. Rather, self-efficacy is domain-specific. People have beliefs about their abilities in specific domains such as computing mathematics, reading, speaking in public, running long distances, playing basketball, and so on. Beliefs about capabilities in one domain do not carry over into another domain unless the domains have similar sub-skills. Because of the domain-specific nature of self-efficacy, the construct should not be confused with a general sense of academic ability or academic self-concept. Self-efficacy deals with people's beliefs about their capabilities on specific tasks.

Why would such a simple mechanism – beliefs about one's capabilities – be so important? This concept and processes associated with it are important because the beliefs that people hold about their capabilities have a profound influence on the subsequent decisions people make and how they experience situations. Bandura's touchstone volume on the construct, summarizing decades of research on self-efficacy in many fields, illustrates the broad implications of the construct. People's beliefs about their capabilities influence the decisions they make, how much effort they exert toward activities, how much they persist in the face of obstacles, how much stress and affective burden they experience during trials, and how they perceive the outcomes of their efforts.[20] In this way, self-efficacy mediates cognitive, affective, motivational, and selective

Table 6.4 Key Points from Self-Efficacy and Sociocultural Theory

Concept	Key ideas	Application points
Self-efficacy	Beliefs about capabilities in specific domains influence people's decisions and how they experience situations.	Exam preparation must build students' beliefs about their capabilities in addition to knowledge and skills.
	Beliefs about capabilities influence motivation, effort, persistence, stress and affective burdens, and expectations of outcomes.	Provide students with mastery experiences in same or similar domains during preparation.
	Beliefs about capabilities are derived from 1) mastery experiences, 2) vicarious experiences, 3) verbal and social persuasion, and 4) physiological and affective states – in various combinations.	Structure for each of these four sources information sources, particularly mastery experiences, in exam supports at both programmatic and classroom levels.
Sociocultural theory	Learning and acquiring skills is connected to developing a new identity in context.	Exam preparation must build a positive test-taker identity in conjunction with skills, content knowledge, and efficacy beliefs.
	How people view themselves as learners in a domain is as important as the skills they develop.	Beliefs about self and one's relationship to licensure exams should guide the design of preparation efforts.
	People need 1) material resources, 2) relational resources, and 3) ideational resources to develop practice-linked identities.	Classroom and programmatic preparation efforts should be built around these three resources.

Source: Author.

processes,[21] each of which is specifically central to academic achievement broadly and teacher licensure exam preparation and performance.

People formulate beliefs about their capabilities from four main sources of information, which are (a) mastery experience, (b) vicarious experience, (c) verbal and social persuasion, and (d) physiological and affective states.[22]

Mastery Experiences

When people have previous mastery experiences (or experiences they appraise to be successful) in a particular domain, they then have a stronger belief in their abilities to successfully complete the same or a similar task. The converse follows from non-mastery (i.e., failure) experiences. Bandura summarizes this point: "Successes build a robust belief in one's personal efficacy. Failures undermine it, especially if failures occur before a sense of efficacy is firmly established."[23] Also important to how one interprets mastery experience with respect to one's efficacy beliefs is the perceived difficulty of the task and the level of effort one expends on that task. People are more likely to draw efficacy beliefs from difficult tasks, and a high level of effort required to achieve a mastery experience can result in decreased efficacy beliefs for some people. Also important to the role of mastery experiences is the framework by which people attribute the cause of their success or failure.[24] For example, when a person attributes success to the ease of a task, this mastery experience will less likely increase self-efficacy. If a person attributes their success to effort, then the mastery experience will more likely increase self-efficacy.

Given the importance of mastery and non-mastery experiences, prior experiences with standardized tests can have a significant influence on beliefs about capabilities on licensure exams. The young adults who enter colleges today are the most tested generation of students in the history of American public education. The tests that saturate their schooling experiences are well beyond the SAT and ACT. They include annual state benchmark tests starting as early as third grade, entrance exams for magnet and charter schools, high school exit exams, college placement tests, and more. Although none of these tests are identical to teacher licensure exams, the high stakes attached to them and the standardized format mean that performance on these can influence initial efficacy beliefs about teacher licensure exams. Consequently, preservice teachers seldom approach licensure exams anew but instead have efficacy beliefs based on prior experiences with other standardized tests.

Vicarious Experience

This second information source refers to the process by which people appraise their own capabilities based on the real and symbolic models of others appraised to be "like them." The thought process goes, "If they can do it, and we are similar, then I can probably do it too." Naturally, the converse logic dealing with failure rather than success also follows from a vicarious experience. When people do not have prior experiences in a task from which to formulate efficacy beliefs, vicarious models become a strong source of information. Additionally, vicarious models that are successful from effort and growth (i.e., a coping model) are more likely to increase efficacy beliefs than successful models through little effort.[25] Importantly, every model does not inherently serve as a vicarious experience that shapes a person's beliefs about their capabilities. People must judge that the model is like them according to important identity markers.

This point about judging that a model is like them is a key point in context with teacher candidates of color. Race remains a salient identity marker in the United States, particularly in academic settings, with intellectual tasks, and in relation to standardized testing. Although there are numerous characteristic and markers by which one can feel likeness and therefore a vicarious experience, race can be a significant one with teacher licensure exams. The scholarship reviewed at the start of this chapter certainly bears this point. Since vicarious models can increase and decrease efficacy beliefs, the salience of race in this manner presents both a challenge and an opportunity to increase success, a point I address below.

Verbal and Social Persuasion

This third information source concerns verbal and other social messages about one's capabilities that people receive. Bandura summarizes that "people who are persuaded verbally that they possess the capabilities to master given tasks are likely to mobilize greater effort and sustain it than if they harbor self-doubts and dwell on personal deficiencies when difficulties arise."[26] Verbal and social persuasion (including self-instruction) should not be understood as simple encouragement from any source. Rather, this information source can increase one's self-efficacy particularly when the recipient of persuasion has reason to believe that the persuader is a reliable judge of the person's abilities *and* the task at hand. While general encouragement is a nice sentiment, it is not likely to significantly increase self-efficacy. Persuasions must come from a valid source of appraisal.

Verbal persuasion alone does not often significantly alter self-efficacy, but people who already possess some stronger reasons to have efficacious beliefs (such as through a prior mastery experience) are more likely to benefit from verbal persuasion.[27]

In view of the nature of verbal and social persuasion with regard to self-efficacy, we can see how inconsequential simple encouragement alone can be in context with licensure exams. Faculty members, friends, and support staff can offer positive support for preservice teachers taking licensure exams, but in order for this support to alter efficacy beliefs, the people giving support must possess certain knowledge. This knowledge includes exam content, passing scores, and administration procedures, as well as the test-taker's skills with respect to these details. We can think here back to the encouragement Shonda received from her mother and grandmother in Chapter 2. Although this support was a kind gesture, from a self-efficacy stance, unless Shonda judged her family members to possess this knowledge, the verbal support likely did not increase her belief in her own capabilities. In order for faculty and staff to be in a position of social and verbal persuasion, they must possess knowledge of both the task and the test-taker's respective abilities. This point identifies one of the weaknesses of simply outsourcing licensure exam support to units outside of teacher education programs, such as remediation centers on campus. Lack of knowledge about the details of licensure exams will undermine how this support can increase self-efficacy.

Physiological and Affective States

As covered in Chapter 5, people experience a variety of emotional and physiological states during tasks. These can include nervousness, anxiety, confusion, fatigue, elevated heart rate, calmness, tranquility, excitement, and more. These states relate to both intellectual and physical tasks. People can interpret these states in different ways. For example, confusion during an academic task or fatigue in an athletic context can be interpreted as indicants of inability. Conversely, with a different cognitive organization, these can also be interpreted as indicators that one is in the process of learning and growing by being challenged. As with mastery experiences, how people interpret physiological and affective states can change the ultimate effect of the information, whether it increases or decreases efficacy beliefs.

With regard to licensure exams and standardized tests more broadly, test-takers can experience many of the physiological and affective states listed above. A particular state, such as nervousness, however, does not necessarily have the same meaning for different test-takers. One test-taker may interpret nervousness as an indicator of inability and unpreparedness. Another may interpret it as a sign of readiness. The ways that people interpret these states can change, so guiding test-takers to interpret states in efficacious ways is important. Separate from the ways these states are described through self-efficacy are the secondary effects of some states, such as the reduction of working memory when people are faced with the threat of confirming a stereotype threat.[28] Although not directly addressed in self-efficacy, these secondary effects are also important.

Summary and Integration of Sources

These four sources of information do not exist separately in people's experiences. Rather, we can draw from these four sources of information in different capacities and combinations to formulate beliefs about our capabilities.[29] However, some information sources take primacy over others. In their review of self-efficacy research, Ellen Usher and Frank Pajares found that mastery experiences often take primacy over the other three information sources and, thus, are consistently the most influential source of information on people's behaviors.[30] We can see evidence of this primacy through the previous chapters when – often first – students talked about their previous experiences with standardized tests and *then* talked about other people's experience or what other people had told them. The work of Bandura supports this conclusion too, in that "enacting mastery experiences are the most influential source of information because they produce the most authentic evidence of whether one can muster whatever it takes to succeed."[31] Vicarious experience, verbal and social persuasions, and emotional and physiological states are also meaningful, often when people do not have mastery experiences in a domain from which to draw. Additionally, all four of these sources interact with one another, and they interact in different ways depending on the specific domain or activity. For example, in an athletic task, a physiological state such as fatigue may be a more powerful information source than verbal or social persuasion. In an academic task such as a standardized mathematics test, a person's prior performance in a mathematics class would likely be a strong influence on their efficacy beliefs. Finally, as with many cognitive functions, the strength of these information sources can vary depending on gender, age, ethnicity, and other salient identity markers. Many psychological surveys, if not most, are validated through samples of white college students in the

United States because they are the most available samples, especially at large, predominantly white research institutions with robust psychology departments. We must consider how what we know about self-efficacy and teacher licensure exams might vary depending upon gender, age, ethnicity, and other salient aspects of identity.

Sociocultural Theory: Identity in Context and "Becoming" a Good Test-Taker

Sociocultural perspectives make up an additional lens that opens up new ways of understanding teacher licensure exams. If self-efficacy focuses on psychological cognitive processes and how people appraise their capabilities, sociocultural theories help unpack aspects of social context and identity that only receive tangential attention due to the cognitive psychological origins of self-efficacy. Scholars typically anchor sociocultural traditions to the work of Lev Vygotsky, and many scholars have extended and sharpened these ideas since his foundational work.[32] Na'ilah Nasir and Victoria Hand provide a rich review of sociocultural theories and their relevance to the intersecting areas of race, culture, and schooling.[33] Within this body of research is the basic but important point that what people do, including the activities they engage in and avoid, are connected to the identities they take on and develop. In this way, how people view themselves as learners in a specific domain (i.e., *practice-linked identities*) is as important as the skills they develop. Additionally, developing skills in a particular domain is related to changes in identity. People take on new roles and new ideas about themselves as they become proficient in areas.[34] From a sociocultural perspective, learning is also about becoming.

Although sociocultural theory is a wide body of scholarship, a few focused points are particularly relevant to the topic of licensure exams. These points deal with the three different types of resources made available to people in learning settings: (a) material resources, (b) relational resources, and (c) ideational resources. These resources are important because people need them to develop identities and skills in specific areas.[35] To illustrate this set of resources, below I draw from a study of track athletes by Nasir and Cooks and, where relevant, make connections to teacher licensure exams and self-efficacy.[36]

Material Resources

Material resources include "the way in which the physical environment, its organization, and the artifacts in it support one's sense of connection to the practice."[37] In work on the development of practice-linked identities in track athletes, Nasir and Cooks indicated that material resources were the track on which practice and meets took place as well as other related items such as appropriate running shoes (i.e., "spikes"), starting blocks, uniforms, hurdlcs, and other items. These material resources were necessary for a track athlete to learn the skills associated with the activity. Equally important, these resources were also necessary in order for an athlete to "become" a runner, sprinter, or hurdler. While the presence of these resources is important, also important is the access that athletes have to them and how they use them.

Material resources are also relevant to learning en route to passing teacher licensure exams. Material resources include test overview documents explaining the content and format of the tests; study materials that contain sample questions, answers, and explanations; and instructional materials that dissect content into basic parts. All of these resources exist in both print and digital forms. Preparation materials for some tests are available *only* in digital form such as e-books, so computers and other electronic devices are also material resources. Consequently, there is a lucrative industry based on these materials. Some students who are well-prepared for tests due to prior schooling experiences do not need these material resources to pass. For students who do not pass licensure exams on their first attempt, or for students who wish to prepare themselves for exams, these materials are necessary.

Material resources highlight an important area not addressed by self-efficacy. In some domains and activities, people need key material resources in order to develop enabling beliefs about their capabilities through mastery experience. If these resources are not available, or if people do not have sufficient access to these resources, then it becomes more difficult to develop mastery experiences and subsequent efficacy beliefs. This point should cause teacher educators to consider how they make preparation materials available to students, the potential unequal distribution of these materials, and the need for institutions to financially invest in student success.

Relational Resources

Relational resources include "the positive relationships with others in the context that can increase connection to the practice."[38] In their study of track athletes, Nasir and Cooks found that relational resources included opportunities to connect with coaches and other athletes on the team. It was particularly important for novices to connect with more advanced athletes on the team, such to the degree that coaches structured for these interactions inside and outside of scheduled practices. These resources were important because it was through them that novices became more connected to the practices of running track. Additionally, it was through relationships with coaches and teammates that athletes became a member of the team, which is the most integral type of community in most sports. These two aspects – connection to track practices and the track team – coincide. The more one becomes part of a team, the most opportunities they have to learn about and develop fundamental skills, correct micro-mistakes, and such.

Relational resources are critical and overlooked dimensions of teacher licensure preparation. Most often, preparation and success for licensure exams is seen only as an individual pursuit, and in some ways, it is. A person typically registers and takes the exam alone, and there is no collective score. Despite these characteristics, relationships between people are central to licensure exams and preparation. Teacher candidates often get their first ideas about the content and level of difficulty of the exam from peers, family members, former teachers, and other people. This information can be subjective and both accurate and inaccurate. These information sources are often more significant in the estimation of students than official information from professors and departmental literature. Chapter 3, with its focus on advice networks and consciously building one, was partly rooted in these ideas about relational resources.

Relational resources also connect directly to the importance of vicarious models of success and verbal persuasion within self-efficacy. Relational resources help create these two information sources of self-efficacy. This emphasis from sociocultural theory brings the relational elements of these sources into focus. What follows is the need to establish the wide dissemination of vicarious models of success and for verbal and social messages that build self-efficacy. At predominantly white universities, teacher candidates of color may have limited contact with other candidates of color who have passed licensure exams. These reasons range from the racial organization of friendship groups, the dynamics in white learning spaces, and the tendency for students who pass their licensure exams (often with ease) to remain quiet about their experiences in order to not seem braggadocios or make other students feel bad. This tendency requires programs to structure for the systemic dissemination of success stories, a topic I discuss in the following chapter.

Ideational Resources

Ideational resources refer to "ideas about oneself and one's relationship to and place in the practice and the world, as well as ideas about what is valued or good."[39] In this way, people hold ideas about themselves with respect to certain activities. These ideas, as heuristics, shape the manners in which people make sense of their experiences in certain domains and the subsequent actions they take. When a person says, "I'm not really a math person," this suggests a set of ideational resources about that person and their relationship to math and its subparts. These ideas can deal with a subjective sense of innate ability, cultural orientation, and more. As with beliefs about capabilities in self-efficacy, ideational resources need not be objectively true to be influential on a person's behavior. The subjective ways that people process experiences have long-term effects on their learning.[40]

Ideational resources are overlooked in the topic of licensure exams but are relevant in two ways. First, a common refrain from some students who do not pass licensure exams is "I'm not a good test-taker." We saw this refrain from Tammy in Chapter 3. Without a doubt, this perspective is objectively true in some cases. Some people are less effective in timed, pressured, and on-demand demonstrations of knowledge and skills. However, separate from the objective reality that one is not a good test-taker is the ideational resource and subjective belief that one is not a good test-taker. In other words, *believing* that one is not a good test-taker shapes how a student prepares for tests (or does not), interprets challenges, and makes sense of successes. Second, some people hold ideational resources about specific domains such as mathematics, writing under pressure, and others. Depending on their content and administration format, licensure exams connect to some of these domains. This point means that teacher educators must attend to the ideational artifacts connected to certain domains and exams, such as all that is signaled by the phrase "I'm just not good at math."

The notion of ideational resources helps reframe ideas from self-efficacy in an important way. Ideational resources push teacher educators to consider the *test-taker identity* that a student holds both in general and in relation to specific domains. And, just as in track, there is a set of ideas about self and abilities that students who do think of themselves as "good test-takers" develop. The information sources from self-efficacy such as previous and vicarious experience help establish this test-taker identity. Once established, this test-taker identity works as a lens through which students interpret their experiences and plan future actions, even if these actions are to avoid learning activities. According to these ideas, in order to support students to pass licensure exams, faculty and staff must work at the level of ideational resources to create positive test-taker identities.

Skills development happens much more easily when these test-taker identities are in place.

Looking Toward Practice

In this chapter, I've outlined two scholarly frameworks and related concepts that give teacher educators specific ways of understanding candidates' experiences with licensure exam. These frameworks help attend to test-taker identity, related practices, information sources from which candidates develop ideas about their capabilities, and more. Frameworks such as these help teacher educators to see that supporting candidates on licensure exams should entail much more than simply doubling down on studying. Supports at both programmatic and classroom scales should address identity as it relates to practice, various kinds of resources, self-efficacy information sources, and more. Anchored to the ideas in this chapter, the next chapter outlines specific practices at programmatic and classroom scales that teacher educators can adopt and adapt into their own contexts.

Notes

1 Albert Bandura, *Self-Efficacy: The Exercise of Self Control* (New York, NY: Worth Publishers, 1997).

2 Na'ilah Suad Nasir and Victoria M. Hand, "Exploring Sociocultural Perspectives on Race, Culture, and Learning," *Review of Educational Research* 76, no. 4 (December 1, 2006): 449–75; Lev Vygotsky, *Mind in Society* (Cambridge, MA: Harvard University Press, 1978).

3 Dan Goldhaber and Michael Hansen, "Race, Gender, and Teacher Testing: How Informative a Tool Is Teacher Licensure Testing?," *American Educational Research Journal* 47, no. 1 (2010): 218–51.

4 Emery Petchauer and Lynnette Mawhinney, *Teacher Education at Minority Serving Institutions: Programs, Policies, and Social Justice* (New Brunswick, NJ: Rutgers University Press, 2017); Clifton Conrad and Marybeth Gasman, *Educating a Diverse Nation: Lessons from Minority Serving Institutions* (Cambridge, MA: Harvard University Press, 2015).

5 Michael T. Nettles et al., *Performance and Passing Rate Differences of African American and White Prospective Teachers on PRAXIS Examinations* (Princeton, NJ: Educational Testing Service, 2011).

6 Linda J. Strassle, "Minimum Competency Testing of Teachers for Certification Due Process Equal Protection and Title Vll Implications," *Cornell Law Review* 70, no. 3 (1985): 494–525.

7 Ibid.

8 Drew H. Gitomer and Andrew S. Latham, "Generalizations in Teacher Education: Seductive and Misleading," *Journal of Teacher Education* 51, no. 3 (2000): 215–20; Goldhaber and Hansen, "Race, Gender, and Teacher Testing"; Dan Goldhaber, "Everyone's Doing It, but What Does Teacher Testing Tell Us about Teacher Effectiveness?," *The Journal of Human Resources* 42, no. 4 (2007): 765–94.

9 Drew H. Gitomer and Andrew S. Latham, "Generalizations in Teacher Education."

10 Drew H. Gitomer, Terran L. Brown, and John Bonett, "Useful Signal or Unnecessary Obstacle? The Role of Basic Skills Tests in Teacher Preparation," *Journal of Teacher Education* 62, no. 5 (2011): 431–45.

11 Ibid, 424.

12 Uri Treisman, "Studying Students Studying Calculus: A Look at the Lives of Minority Mathematics Students in College," *The College Mathematics Journal* 23, no. 5 (1992): 362–72.

13 Charles T. Clotfelter, Helen F. Ladd, and Jacob L. Vigdor, "Teacher-Student Matching and the Assessment of Teacher Effectiveness," *Journal of Human Resources* 41, no. 4 (1974): 778–820.

14 Goldhaber, "Everyone's Doing It."

15 Ibid, 778.

16 Ibid, "Race, Gender, and Teacher Testing."

17 Ibid, 238.

18 Albert Bandura, "Self-Efficacy: Toward a Unifying Theory of Behavioral Change," *Psychological Review* 84, no. 2 (1977): 191–215.

19 Albert Bandura, *Self-Efficacy: The Exercise of Self Control*, 3.

20 Ellen L. Usher and Frank Pajares, "Sources of Self-Efficacy in School: Critical Review of the Literature and Future Directions," *Review of Educational Research* 78, no. 4 (2008): 751–96.

21 Albert Bandura, *Self-Efficacy: The Exercise of Self Control*.

22 Ellen L. Usher and Frank Pajares, "Sources of Self-Efficacy in School"; Albert Bandura, *Self-Efficacy: The Exercise of Self Control*.

23 Albert Bandura, *Self-Efficacy: The Exercise of Self Control*, 80.

24 Barnard Weiner, *An Attributional Theory of Motivation and Emotion* (New York, NY: Springer, 1986).

25 Alan E. Kazdin, "Covert Modeling and the Reduction of Avoidance Behavior," *Journal of Abnormal Psychology* 81, no. 1 (1973): 87–95; Donald H. Meichenbaum, "Examination of Model Characteristics in Reducing Avoidance Behavior," *Journal of Personality and Social Psychology* 17, no. 3 (1971): 298–307.

26 Albert Bandura, *Self-Efficacy: The Exercise of Self Control*, 101.

27 Catherine A. Chambliss and Edward J. Murray, "Efficacy Attribution, Locus of Control, and Weight Loss," *Cognitive Therapy and Research* 3, no. 4 (1979): 349–53.

28 Toni Schmader and Michael Johns, "Converging Evidence That Stereotype Threat Reduces Working Memory Capacity," *Journal of Personality and Social Psychology* 85, no. 3 (2003): 440–52.

29 Albert Bandura, *Self-Efficacy: The Exercise of Self Control*.

30 Ellen L. Usher and Frank Pajares, "Sources of Self-Efficacy in School."

31 Albert Bandura, *Self-Efficacy: The Exercise of Self Control*, 80.

32 Michael Cole, *Cultural Psychology: A Once and Future Discipline* (Cambridge, MA: Harvard University Press, 1996); Jean Lave and Etienne Wenger, *Situated Learning:*

Legitimate Peripheral Participation, 1st edition (Cambridge, UK: Cambridge University Press, 1991); James E. Cote and Charles G. Levine, *Identity, Formation, Agency, and Culture: A Social Psychological Synthesis* (Mahwah, NJ: Psychology Press, 2002).

33 Na'ilah Suad Nasir and Victoria M. Hand, "Exploring Sociocultural Perspectives."

34 Lave and Wenger, *Situated Learning*; Etienne Wenger, *Communities of Practice: Learning, Meaning, and Identity*, 1st edition (Cambridge, UK: Cambridge University Press, 1999).

35 James E. Cote and Charles G. Levine, *Identity, Formation, Agency, and Culture.*

36 Na'ilah Suad Nasir and Jamal Cooks, "Becoming a Hurdler: How Learning Settings Afford Identities," *Anthropology & Education Quarterly* 40, no. 1 (2009): 41–61.

37 Ibid, 47.

38 Ibid, 47.

39 Ibid, 47.

40 David S. Yeager and Gregory M. Walton, "Social-Psychological Interventions in Education: They're Not Magic," *Review of Educational Research* 81, no. 2 (2011): 267–301.

People Pass All the Time

7

Promising Practices for Teacher Educators

The previous chapter introduced two frameworks and related concepts through which teacher educators can understand teacher licensure exams for preservice teachers. This final chapter outlines specific practices that generate from these frameworks. I outline practices at both programmatic and classroom levels that teacher educators can implement in their own contexts. The practices I describe below deal with the beliefs, heuristics, and subjective ideas that inform performance and skills development. In other words, faculty members wishing to support preservice teachers should address identities in context, related practices, beliefs about capabilities, and other processes. Like any set of recommendations, readers should consider how these coordinate with the specific culture, context, and student populations of their institutions.

Programmatic Level Practices

Teacher education programs should institute supports at programmatic levels. Here, I refer to the policies that guide students' actions, shape the experiences they have, and connect them to other groups. Some of these policies and practices facilitate certain advice networks or vicarious models of success, two topics discussed in previous chapters. Other priorities at programmatic levels increase the likelihood of mastery experiences.

Timing

There is a common sentiment that students should take licensure exams as soon as they express an interest in teaching, normally during their first semester in college if possible. Similarly, some students elect to take the exam unprepared under the guise of "just to see what it is like," as was the case with some students in previous chapters. These approaches risk giving students – if they are not adequately prepared for the test – an initial failure experience with the exam that can substantially lower self-efficacy, reinforce or establish a negative test-taker identity, and shape students' subsequent actions and experiences with the exam in negative ways. Instead of taking the exam as soon as possible or just to see what it is like, students should take the exam as soon as they are gauged to be ready. In order to gauge this readiness, faculty members must be deeply familiar with the test (by taking it themselves) and by engaging with students in preparation activities.

One important qualifier with this recommendation is that undergraduate programs must identify their students who wish to become teachers early and work with them to prepare for licensure exams. In undergraduate programs, if faculty members do not come in contact with these students until their second year in college, then a year of preparation time has been lost, and students then have a smaller window of time to prepare and pass. (Post-baccalaureate programs that accept a certain number of students do not experience this dynamic.) Consequently, programs must develop high-contact advising systems that are informed about licensure requirements and make early contact with students. Simply abiding by the principle that students should take the exam as early as possible can be an excuse for a poor advising system and ultimately disadvantage teacher candidates, especially ones who enter programs with negative experiences with standardized tests and will be more likely to delay taking the exam.

These ideas about timing concern when in a student's matriculation they should take the exam. Teacher educators should also consider specific times during a semester and the affordances and constraints of those times. Many states now allow for candidates to take exams in computerized formats at test centers connected to or independent from institutions. In this format, candidates can simply make an appointment for a day and time that works in their schedule. Planning ahead, teacher educators can organize their candidates to make their appointments during times of the semester, such as spring or fall break, that are typically less demanding with academic work. This time period is ideal – not so candidates can cram the week of the exam but because their cognitive and affective load is likely lower. We saw Destiny in Chapter 2 allude to this benefit the final time she passed her exam. The rolling appointments of computerized test centers also allow for programs to collectivize what is usually an individual process. Candidates working together in workshop cohorts can register to take their exam on the same day or in the same two or three-day window. This collective scheduling can create comradery and reduce feelings of isolation. In instances when candidates have to take a paper-and-pencil exam during one of a few specified date options, faculty members can still organize students to take the exam during the same sitting.

Structuring for Mastery

Programs must also systematically structure for students to have mastery experiences in domains that students judge to be similar to licensure exams. As I discussed in the previous chapter, mastery experiences are consistently the strongest sources of efficacy beliefs. Consequently, as programs are preparing students for their licensure exams, they must provide students with opportunities for early and frequent mastery experiences. These experiences need not be with extensive and full sample tests. Instead, singular items or items in small groups are better because they reduce the possibility that students will interpret practice items as failure experiences. It is important for students to understand that these activities are aligned with licensure exam content, too. If students do not appraise exercises to be similar to exam content, then the exercises will less likely increase self-efficacy. Finally, when students have these mastery experiences, it is critical that they attribute their success to their own efforts.[1] Faculty and staff can scaffold this attribution by metacognitive activities and cuing questions that ask students to identify the source of their mastery and improvement. Quantitatively charting student growth is an additional way to scaffold for this attribution. Finally, the manner in which faculty members talk about right and wrong answers can support this growth. I say more about this point in the classroom section below.

One way to quickly and accidentally undermine mastery experience is to give students a lengthy diagnostic test that mirrors the length of an actual teacher licensure exam. Although it is important to diagnose what skills students may need to develop, long diagnostic tests can simultaneously function as an initial, crushing failure experience that will lower self-efficacy and reinforce a negative test-taker identity. As stated above, these experiences will then undermine preparation efforts. Diagnosis is necessary, but programs should accomplish it in the most minimal way possible. For example, if a student answers only four out of ten geometry questions correctly, there is no need to have them answer eight out of twenty correctly, or sixteen out of forty. The need for skills development is sufficiently established after five questions.

Furthermore, misunderstanding the design of standardized tests can decrease self-efficacy for students. Occasionally, I have seen high-achieving students who have entered college with Advanced Placement credit in English have their test efficacy shaken because of a lengthy diagnostic reading test in which they scored 75% correct. This is typically a strong passing score on licensure exams due to the test design for a large distribution of scores. But, few students know this facet of test design; therefore, they expect to score around 90% correct because their grades in English courses are usually around 90%. Consequently, they misunderstand the score as an indicant of inability, and it decreases their self-efficacy. This misunderstanding can also suggest to students that licensure exams are somehow fundamentally different from the material they have previously encountered in their years of schooling, an incorrect assumption that increases anxiety. In some of these cases, students might have been better off not taking a diagnostic test and simply taking the exam with their high self-efficacy, as Brandon did in Chapter 5. The potential for misunderstanding requires that faculty members must clearly explain to students the nature and design of diagnostic tests before students take the tests and see scores.

Faculty members should also consider the tradeoffs of sharing (or not sharing) diagnostic results with students. Sharing poor performance on a diagnostic test gives students an accurate picture of where they stand, but it can also lower self-efficacy. In some instances, it may be fruitful for faculty members to design growth experiences for a student based upon their diagnostic results but without sharing those results with students, or perhaps waiting until the student develops a more sturdy test-taker identity further into preparation before sharing those diagnostic results.[2]

Structuring for Vicarious Experience and Relevant Social Interaction

There are also specific efforts that programs can take to structure for important vicarious experiences and social interactions that increase self-efficacy. From a sociocultural perspective, these vicarious experiences are relational resources to develop test-taker identities. Essentially, programs must develop ways to disseminate these models and stories to students who have not yet taken licensure exams. One way to do this is by involving these successful students in the preparation process of other classmates. For example, peer tutoring or using students who have passed as aides during preparation workshops or labs allows other students to see that passing is not an anomaly. These vicarious models are particularly important for students of color if students "like them" are not highly visible. They see that people like them pass all the time. A second way to accomplish this vicarious experience is to take short video profiles of students who have passed their exams. Students can talk about their experiences, discuss what they did to be successful, and give advice to future test-takers. With permission, the names and photographs of students who have passed can also be put on a space of recognition, such as a department bulletin board or website, for all to see. The robust professional learning that happens through regular hashtag Twitter chats can also be instructive here. Programs can archive and make accessible success narratives by associating them with a hashtag connected to their program.

With each of these means of dissemination, the importance is not the content that students give, such as the specific advice to future test-takers. While this advice may be beneficial, the primary purpose is to illustrate to teacher candidates that students "just like them" have passed the examination. To some readers, these may seem like redundant or unnecessary efforts. However, students who pass exams have many reasons not to talk about their successes voluntarily. If surrounded by other students who are struggling with passing, talking about success may appear insensitive.

Reluctance to talk about success can work a bit differently for candidates of color, especially in predominantly white programs and institutions. For teacher candidates of color, talking about their success (again, in a predominantly white context) may elicit disbelief or surprise from white classmates and professors who hold racist stereotypes and thus did not expect them to be successful. Even a genuine, overly-enthusiastic "Wow, congratulations!" can signal that the speaker had lower expectations for a test-taker.[3] For Asian American students subject to racist stereotypes about intelligence and mathematics, sharing their success (or struggles) can subject them to racist comments that make them uncomfortable. Consequently, reluctance about sharing success and intentionally staying out of sight can be strategies to avoid racist and uncomfortable comments for prospective teachers of color.

The outcome of these understandable tactics, however, is impressions that fewer candidates pass licensure exams. Essentially, activities to disseminate vicarious models of success are to create a culture of celebration for licensure exam achievement that still protects students of color from racism or hypervisibility. What helps establish this culture is explaining to students why it is important to talk about their experiences and that doing so can demystify the exam and boost the confidence of other students. By reframing the topic in this way – and being careful not to replicate deficit or stereotypical assumptions indirectly – students feel freer to talk about their successes and challenges without fear of appearing as if they are bragging or insensitive to other students' difficulties.

With these vicarious models, it is also important to have models that have been successful through much effort (i.e., coping models) and not just models that have been successful on their first attempt. Coping models are found in students who struggled or failed on their first attempt and then passed after studying and applying diligent preparation, like each of the women profiled in Chapter 2. These types of models are different from ones who are successful on their first attempt without much preparation. These coping models are important because they illustrate that one *can* improve with effort and that skill is neither fixed nor inherent.[4] Models that are successful with little effort can be understood by some students as simply possessing some innate ability to perform well. Both of these models are beneficial. First-time success models, especially for minoritized groups, counter the stereotype that they are not "naturally" good at standardized tests. Coping models, which are more often overlooked, illustrate that one can improve with effort even if they initially struggle.

To illustrate the different types of models for students, I will often give them three different score reports from their peers (with test-takers' permission). These score reports will illustrate a student who passed the first time and then two cases of students who passed on multiple attempts. From the score reports, students can see the time separating attempts and that the score increased over time. In many instances, the students whose score reports were passed out would come to the workshop and explain the efforts they took between test sittings to improve their scores. Very importantly, I would communicate that the struggles students experience with standardized tests are not unique to any fixed, essential aspect of their identity such as ethnicity, gender, and so on. In fact, the struggles are not unique to any specific group. Rather, all types of people get nervous and might struggle with standardized tests and licensure exams. Having sample scores from a racially diverse group also communicates this point indirectly. Additionally for some activities, students are in racially mixed groups so they see that successes and struggles are not limited to any specific group. Getting students to internalize the belief that all different types of people might struggle is a psychological intervention with widespread positive effects.[5]

Classroom Level Practices

The classroom level practices discussed in this section address developing positive test-taker identity through ideational resources. What ideas guide people who believe that they are "good test-takers?" What ideas about self and one's relationship to licensure exams are healthy? I outline answers to questions like these under headings that represent the ideational resources I've often said directly to individuals and groups. I have put the subheadings below in quotations because teacher educators can speak them in the social learning environment.

"The Test Can't Change Who You Are"

Because of the importance of teacher licensure exams, some students see and experience their performance as a defining characteristic of their lives in college. We saw some indicators of this perspective from Tammy in Chapter 3. The licensure exam was a fulcrum around which all her experienced moved. This is a natural association given the gatekeeping position that these tests occupy and that the college years are usually a significant time of personal growth and change. Research suggests that students are more susceptible to stereotype and identity threats when exams matter a great deal and are important to them.[6] In light of this, it is crucial that test-takers internalize the idea that neither the test nor their performance fundamentally change who they are. Getting students to internalize this idea has a number of benefits. It alleviates some of the pressure associated with test performance, makes students less susceptible to stereotype and identity threats, and makes them more able to access skills and knowledge during the exams.

This point can be conveyed to students with humor. For example, if you are a rotten person before the test and get every question right, you are still a rotten person. Or, if you are a kind and loving person before the test and answer every question wrong, you are still a kind and loving person after the test. A test cannot positively or negatively define who you are. These are the kinds of perspectives I often verbalize to students while discussing the exam and, at the same time, I try to shift the ways they think about their relationship with the exam. Internalizing this idea takes place not only by talking about it but by value affirmation: having students affirm the values and qualities that they hold to be central to who they are. Successful intervention studies have students complete short writing exercises in which they write about the values that are important to their lives and why they matter.[7] With these students, instead of studying the night before the exam, they complete these types of writing exercises. In Chapter 2, Heather referenced the benefit of these exact exercises as she prepared to retake her exam.

"You Can Work Under Pressure"

Another key ideational resource is working well under pressure. A common refrain among students who struggle on licensure exams is that they could complete the work if they had more time. For them, the content of the exam is not an issue. The issue is additional pressure of completing the items in a limited timeframe. Students with a positive test-taker identity believe they can complete tasks in a timed, pressured situation. When students internalize this belief, it helps them to be calmer during the test event as well as access knowledge and skills that they possess. As with all of these ideational resources, talking about them in the learning environment so that they become part of the common discourse is a subtle but powerful way for students to internalize them. I often tell students, "You *can* work well under pressure." To coincide with this discourse, I gradually and gently impose time limits on practice activities in courses and tutorials so that over time students have experiential proof that they *can* work well in timed-pressure situations. Finally, when students demonstrate resilience, persistence, and levels of success under timed settings, highlighting their success in timed settings is vital. This practice helps them recognize growth and attribute new successes to their own effort and progress, not something external and out of their control like chance or luck.

"If They Can Do It, You Can Do It"/"People Like You Pass All the Time"

The ideational resources in these quotations derive from vicarious models of success that increase self-efficacy. As I discussed in the previous chapter, when people have high self-efficacy beliefs in specific domains, they are more likely to engage rather than avoid preparation activities, more likely to exert effort during a challenge, and less likely to process struggles as indicators of inability.[8] The programmatic recommendations in the previous section are structural ways to provide successful vicarious experiences, but changing the narrative and discourse of learning spaces and workshops around licensure exams can have this outcome as well. "People like you pass all the time" is a refrain that helps organize the value of learning activities. The phrase can be of value alone, but talking about specific students' experiences (with their permission) or having them talk about their experiences with other students adds specificity to the claim.

One powerful indicator that ideational resources such as these have become part of the learning environment and are shifting the narrative is when students begin saying them to one another. I saw a clear example of this shift one year during the routine of students who had passed the exam putting on a panel discussion that gave advice to students who were preparing to take the exam. Tamara, who took two attempts to pass the math portion of her exam, told the group, "I'm horrible at math, and I passed. So if I can do it, *you* can do it. People pass all the time." Of course, it's not desirable that Tamara would think of herself as "horrible" at math (in fact, she exceeded the required passing score when she passed). But for other students who also thought of themselves as horrible at math, she served as a powerful vicarious example of success. Someone "like them" in low appraisement of math can pass.

"Half and Some Change to Pass"

Standardized tests are usually designed for a large distribution of scores. For this and other reasons, this means that approximately 60% correct is usually a passing score on a licensure exam, with some variation depending on the precise exam and what score a particular state sets as a cutoff. That a passing score is a little more than half correct is a foreign concept to students. When students are asked what percentage they think they need to get correct in order to pass, they normally guess 90% since this figure has represented a "good grade" in most of their schooling experiences. They are then shocked to learn that a passing score is typically a bit more than half. The phrase "half and some change" is a succinct way to communicate the passing score and their goal. The goal is not to get all questions right, as is typically the case on tests in class. The goal is usually not even to get 80% right. In fact, trying to get these high percentages correct in a licensure exam might actually undermine student success since they would push themselves to work each problem and thus budget time poorly. The goal is to get half and some change.[9]

Focusing on only this passing mark rather than scoring the highest one might sound like setting a low standard for students. However, most students intuit what scholarly findings suggest: that licensure exams are only marginal indicators of their future teaching effectiveness. Focusing on only the passing scores takes some needless pressure off of students in both preparation and the test. With this in mind, when students encounter a question that they do not understand while taking the test, this mantra gives them freedom to make an educated guess about the answer rather than expend valuable cognitive and affective energy trying to solve it. This mantra also makes the affective implications much less severe for a handful of questions that a student did not understand and possibly answered incorrectly. A student can get one third of the test incorrect and still pass. Additionally, when students spend less time on questions that they might not answer correctly and more time on the ones that they will, they experience less confusion and frustration during the test. Finally, it is simply a more effective use of time for students to spend minutes on questions they are more likely to answer correctly. As with other recommendations in this section, this refrain becomes part of the learning environment through repetition. While going over and reviewing the basic requirements of the test, I have often used the phrase "half and some change" to describe a passing score. When asking students what their goal is, they respond "half and some change." Some students I know even mentally repeat the phrase during the test when they encounter a confounding question as a reminder to make an educated guess, mark the question for review at the end, and move on without wasting time.

"One Question at a Time"

Some students feel that the entire weight of the whole exam is on each question. Or worse, some students feel the weight of *multiple* exams on each question. A more productive mindset is to view each question as a singular exercise bracketed from the rest of the exam: "one question at a time." When students view the test and items in this way, it decreases the overall pressure they experience. Students are able to focus on the specific task at hand and access relevant knowledge and skills rather than think about what questions are next or feel the pressure of the entire exam. Taking the exam one question at a time also makes the implications of a wrong answer less severe. From time to time, students finish the remainder of an exam with little thought and effort after a sequence of particularly startling or confusing questions. The sequences of tough questions breaks their will and they submit thought and effort to the exam. In one extreme case, a student once told me that she thoughtlessly bubbled in the remaining questions of a math test after the first questions stumped her. The miniature failure on a single question can influence students' level of effort, attention, and engagement with the rest of the exam if they do not bracket each question from the rest.

One way to have students internalize this ideational resource is not only to say it frequently in the learning environment but to use it to frame practice on test items. As students complete groups of practice questions, I often tell them not to think ahead to other items. And, once they answer a question and fill in its respective answer bubble, they are to forget about that question and move on. They are to take the test one question at a time.

"There's No Test You Can't Pass"

One final ideational resource of strong test-taker identity is the belief that "there's no test you can't pass." An important qualification to this belief is passing in due time and with the right level of preparation. In other words, one does not pass simply by taking a test over and over. A person passes with adequate preparation. Internalizing this belief makes students more likely to take part in preparation activities, exert effort in the midst of challenge, and ultimately attribute success to their themselves. Similar to other recommendations in this chapter, the narrative about licensure exams in the learning environment helps students to internalize this resource. Also, it is useful having students consider other things in their lives at which they were not initially good or proficient but somehow did become good or proficient. Scaffolding for this thought process, I've often asked students, how did this happen? How did they get from bad to good, from non-proficient to proficient in other kinds of specific domains or activities they named? Students see from this line of questioning that having opportunities to practice, receiving feedback, and exerting effort are what makes one better, no matter what the domain. Understanding this point also helps students to see that they often tacitly construct licensure exams as a "one shot deal," which is much different from how they understand growth and achievement in other domains. I often then ask students how far they are willing to go in order to pass an exam and what they are willing to sacrifice to do so. This line of questioning, either verbally or through short writing exercises, usually helps students focus on the belief that there is no test they cannot pass.

Conclusions and Caveats

A critical caveat for all the recommendations discussed above deals with the indirect, subtle, and stealthy nature of them. The design and purpose of program and classroom interventions should not be made explicit to students. A useful explanation of this point comes from David Yeager and Gregory Walton in their discussion of lasting social psychological interventions; they noted that successful interventions that increase performance, especially for minoritized groups, are neither overt nor heavy-handed. Changing psychological processes "sometimes requires a lighter touch."[10] Using an example from the previous section, it would not be appropriate to tell a teacher candidate of color who is preparing for their licensure exams that because of their assumed low self-efficacy, they are going to be tutored by another student of color for the purpose of increasing their self-efficacy. This explicit presentation of the purpose of the activity decreases its effectiveness by taking students' attention *away* from their own actions, capabilities, and improvements. Displacing this attention also runs the risk of stigmatizing students and replicating deficit assumptions. Claude Steele discussed similar phenomena, such as over-encouraging students.[11] He examined how this can cue stereotype threats about abilities or cause students to question their abilities. The thought process goes, "Is my teacher encouraging me so much because they actually think I'm less likely to be successful? Is this encouragement because they actually think I can't do it?" Due to these unforeseen effects, the kinds of practices I've discussed in this chapter should be precise and deliberate, but they must also be subtle.

Notes

1 Barnard Weiner, *An Attributional Theory of Motivation and Emotion* (New York, NY: Springer, 1986).
2 I'm grateful to Nick Hartlep at Metropolitan State University for sharing this point with me.
3 Claude M. Steele, *Whistling Vivaldi: How Stereotypes Affect Us and What We Can Do* (New York, NY: W.W. Norton, 2010).

4 Alan E. Kazdin, "Covert Modeling and the Reduction of Avoidance Behavior," *Journal of Abnormal Psychology* 81, no. 1 (1973): 87–95; Donald H. Meichenbaum, "Examination of Model Characteristics in Reducing Avoidance Behavior," *Journal of Personality and Social Psychology* 17, no. 3 (1971): 298–307.

5 David S. Yeager and Gregory M. Walton, "Social-Psychological Interventions in Education: They're Not Magic," *Review of Educational Research* 81, no. 2 (2011): 267–301.

6 Claude M. Steele, *Whistling Vivaldi: How Stereotypes Affect Us and What We Can Do.*

7 Geoffrey L. Cohen et al., "Reducing the Racial Achievement Gap: A Social-Psychological Intervention," *Science* 313, no. 5791 (2006): 1307–10; Andy Martens et al., "Combating Stereotype Threat: The Effect of Self-Affirmation on Women's Intellectual Performance," *Journal of Experimental Social Psychology* 42, no. 2 (2006): 236–43.

8 Albert Bandura, *Self-Efficacy: The Exercise of Self Control* (New York, NY: Worth Publishers, 1997).

9 This point, quite clearly, may vary depending on the specific psychometric design of a particular exam. The mantra can simply change to approximate what is roughly passing on a particular exam.

10 David S. Yeager and Gregory M. Walton, "Social-Psychological Interventions in Education," 285.

11 Claude M. Steele, *Whistling Vivaldi: How Stereotypes Affect Us and What We Can Do.*

Appendix A
Interview Protocols

Interview Protocol 1

This protocol was designed to understand reasons for significant score increases (Chapter 2). Ideas from sociocultural theory and self-efficacy informed its design.

1. Generally speaking, what do you think made the difference the time you passed?

Changes in Preparation and Study Habits

2. What was your mindset like when studying the time you passed the exam? Was it different from the time you didn't pass the exam?
3. What was your preparation like before the time you passed compared to the time you didn't pass? Did you do anything differently to prepare before the time you passed?

Changes in Efficacy-Related Sources of Information

4. What was your study experience like before the time you passed? Were you getting questions right or wrong? How did you make sense of that? (Mastery experiences.)
5. Between the time you passed and didn't pass, did you meet more people who had passed or study with more people who had passed? (Relational resources and vicarious models of success.)

6. Did you have people around you telling you things about your abilities or encouraging you? (Verbal and social persuasion; Relational resources.)

Changes in Access to Practice-Linked Identity Resources

7. Did you get new study materials or resources before the time you passed? If so, what were they, and how did you use them? (Material resources.)
8. Did your perspective on the test change at all compared to the time you didn't pass? (Ideational resources.)
9. Did you learn anything new about the test in that time period before you passed it? (e.g., to not leave any question blank). (Ideational resources.)
10. Did your perspectives of **yourself** or your **abilities** change between the times you took the exam? (Ideational resources; self-efficacy beliefs.)

Experiencing the Test Event

11. Did you do anything differently while taking the exam the time you passed? (e.g., managing time, guessing).
12. Did you feel differently while taking the exam the time you passed? How did it feel compared to the time you didn't pass?
13. When you saw questions that you didn't know, what did you think and how did you feel?
14. When you saw questions that you did know, what did you think and how did you feel?

Looking Beyond Praxis

15. How do you feel now that you passed Praxis? Has this experience changed your outlook on yourself or your skills? If so, how?

Interview Protocol 2

This protocol was designed to understand students' experiences with their licensure exam – both thinking about it and the "test event" of taking the exam. The protocol also attends to beliefs about their capabilities on the exam and beliefs about cultural bias.

1. What are your general feelings about standardized tests? (Probe: What standardized tests have you taken?)
2. Scroll Exercise 1: What words come to mind when you hear the word "Praxis?" (This question was printed on a scroll size sticky note, and students wrote their responses in marker before discussing them as a group.)
3. Before you took Praxis, how did you predict your performance would be? (i.e., How did you think you would do?) (Probes: on the whole thing? On individual tests?)
4. What accounts for your prediction on Praxis? (Probes: classes, other tests, what others have said?)
5. What kinds of things did you do to prepare for Praxis, if anything at all?
6. Scroll Exercise 2: What words describe how you felt while actually taking Praxis? (Can include before, during, and after the test; same instructions as Question 2 above.)
7. How was your experience with Praxis similar to and/or different from other standardized tests you have taken?
8. What do you think is most difficult about Praxis? (Probes: time limits, content, format?)
9. A lot of people say that these tests are culturally biased or that they favor some groups over others. To what extent do you agree or disagree with this?
10. Some research shows that minority students perform lower on standardized tests compared to majority or white students. What do you think are some reasons for this performance? (Probes: Are stereotype threat and vulnerability factors?)
11. Are there any other parts of the Praxis test that you want to bring up or that you think we should talk about? (Open-ended portion of interview.)

Interview Protocol 3

This protocol was designed to understand students' experiences with their licensure exam – both thinking about it and the "test event" of taking the exam. The protocol also attends to potential triggers in the test space and their beliefs about standardized test-taking abilities.

1. What are your general opinions about standardized tests?
2. Scroll Exercise 1: What words come to mind when you hear the word "Praxis?" (This question was printed on a scroll size sticky note, and

students wrote their responses in marker before discussing them as a group.)

3. Before you took Praxis, how did you predict your performance would be? (i.e., How did you think you would do?) (Probes: on the whole thing? On individual tests?)

4. What accounts for your prediction on Praxis? (Probes: classes, other tests, what others have said?)

5. What kinds of things did you do to prepare for Praxis, if anything at all?

6. Scroll Exercise 2: What words describe how you felt while actually taking Praxis? (Can include before, during, and after the test; same instructions as Question 2 above.)

7. Were there any instances during the test where mood or mindset quickly changed? You were thinking or feeling one way, and then something made you think or feel differently?

8. At what points during the day were you most uncomfortable, and at what times were you most comfortable?

9. Some people believe that people are just born good standardized test-takers, and other people believe that you can become a good standardized test-taker by practice and effort. What are your beliefs and opinions about people's standardized test-taking abilities? (Prompt: have your beliefs and opinions changed over time?)

10. Do you have any questions for me?

Appendix B
Advice Network Survey

Licensure Exam Survey

Date: _____
Part One: Please complete the following information

1. Name:
2. Gender:
3. Age:
4. Race/ethnicity:
5. University:

   a. Transferred? Y/N

6. # Semesters in school:
7. Cumulative GPA (estimate if you are unsure):
8. List all the dates (MM/YY) and scores (estimate if you can't recall) of your previous Praxis exams:
9. When was the first time you heard about the Praxis exam? (circle one)

   a. Middle school
   b. High school
   c. 1st year of college
   d. 2nd year of college

10. How many people do you know who have passed Praxis? (circle one)

   a. None
   b. 1–2
   c. 4–9
   d. 10+

11. Do you participate in any regular study groups? If so, please list them.
12. Who are the top three people who have influenced your feelings about and preparation for Praxis? List them in order of influence.

Part Two: Network members
In the first column of the attached table, list up to ten key people who have shared information with you about the Praxis exam. 'Information' can include stories about their own or others' experiences taking the exam, things they've heard from other people, logistical information (such as how to apply to take the test), how difficult or easy it is, etc.

For each key person listed, answer the following questions, marking your responses in the corresponding columns on the table (see sample response for example).

1. Gender

   a. Male
   b. Female

2. Age (to the best of your knowledge)

   a. 0–16
   b. 17–22
   c. 23–28
   d. 29–35
   e. 36–45
   f. 45+

3. Race/ethnicity (choose all that apply)

   a. Black/African American
   b. Hispanic
   c. White/Caucasian
   d. Asian/Pacific Islander
   e. Native American
   f. Other

4. Types of information this person offers (choose all that apply)

   a. Advice
   b. Personal experiences
   c. Logistics

d. Level of difficulty / ease

e. Test-taking strategies

f. Information about other people's experiences

g. Other _____

5. How often do you communicate with this person about Praxis? (choose one)

a. Only once or twice a week

b. Few times a semester

c. Couple times a month

d. Once a week

e. More than once a week

6. How well do you know this person? (choose one)

1	2	3	4	5
(not very well) (friend-of-a-friend)		(somewhat well) (classmate)		(very well) (close friend)

7. How influential has this person been on your feelings about Praxis?

1	2	3	4	5
(not at all)	(not very)	(somewhat)	(influential)	(very influential)

8. How influential has this person been on your preparation for Praxis?

1	2	3	4	5
(not at all)	(not very)	(somewhat)	(influential)	(very influential)

9. How has this person influenced your sense of confidence about passing Praxis?

1	2	3	4	5
(must less confident)	(less confident)	(neutral)	(more confident)	(much more confident)

10. In what contexts have you communicated with this person about Praxis? (choose all that apply)

   a. Social gathering
   b. Academic courses
   c. Advising meetings
   d. Study group
   e. Private conversation
   f. Online (Facebook, Twitter, etc.)
   g. Information sessions
   h. Other _____

Your Name _____

Names of information providers	1.Gender	2.Age	3.Race/eth	4.Infooffered	5.Communication	6.Closeness	7.Influence on feelings	8.Influence on preparation	9.Influence on confidence	10.Contexts of communication
[Example] John Doe	A	C	B	B, A, and E	C	2	3	2	2	A, E, and F

Your Name _____

Part Three: The Network
Write the names of the key people you have listed in the table, in the circles below. Then, draw arrows between the circles to indicate who shares information with whom. See the example on the following page.

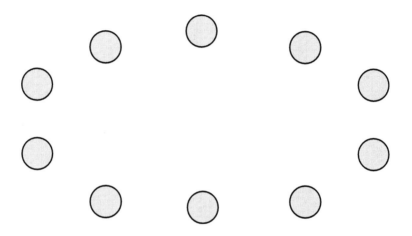

Example network drawing:

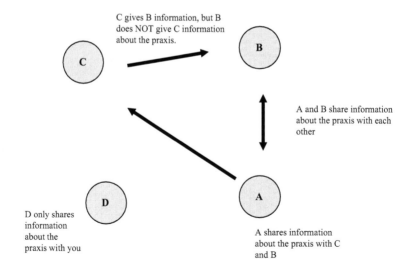

Index